Spaces in Architecture

Spaces in Architecture

Areas, Distances, Dimensions

Bert Bielefeld

Birkhäuser

Basel

Contents

1 Introduction

When transforming a design concept into a feasible project, architects constantly need information on space requirements and room sizes as well as the dimensions of furnishings and their required clearances. Each design task involves spaces with general requirements, such as corridors and sanitary facilities, and others with sometimes highly specific demands, like the surgical unit of a hospital.

This book details the fundamentals and planning basics for various room types that are valid for a diverse assortment of typologies. These are treated systematically, with attention given to their requirements, functional relationships, and detailed dimensional specifications.

Preceding the section on the distinct room types, the chapter "Human Measure" details the requirements placed on buildings by the "average person" and by people with impairments or disabilities. For the purposes of promoting universal design, issues pertaining to barrier-free accessibility are integrated throughout the entire book.

The book *Spaces in Architecture* may be seen as an excerpt from the book *Planning Architecture,* which goes beyond the individual spaces to present detailed design approaches for various typologies. *Spaces in Architecture* is intended to serve in a complementary manner as a handy reference guide for convenient use when designing. It goes without saying that a functional approach does not replace the creative and highly individual design processes of architects. It should, however, offer the possibility to directly combine design ideas with functional requirements.

Individual design approaches and the contents of drawings must always be adapted to relevant national or regional standards. Due to this great diversity of requirements, no guarantee can be made for the applicability of the dimensions and conditions specified here. The dimensions and clearances presented in this book are therefore to be understood as a design aid and not as binding in a legal or normative sense. Moreover, dimensions that are identified as minimum requirements should be freely adjusted if needed to achieve comfortable conditions.

2 Human Measure

Our built environment is designed according to the requirements of the people using it. Consequently, room sizes, heights, and transitions as well as the operating elements such as switches, handles, furniture, etc. must be coordinated with human proportions and dimensions – anthropometry – and human ergonomics.

All kinds of dimensional relationships can be derived from people's motor skills. The resultant minimum space requirements for various routine movement sequences and everyday situations at work and at leisure are thus universal. Since the dimensions relate to people's movement capabilities, special user groups – such as small children, the elderly, and wheelchair users – must be considered when planning.

When dimensioning areas where many people will congregate, an important factor for the design and planning is how that area will be used. For example, communication areas like the lobby in front of a concert hall require significantly more area per person than do access control points where groups of people wait to pass through.

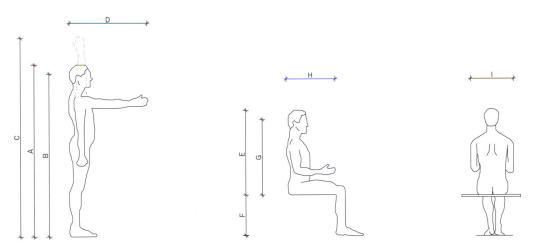

Figure 2.1   Planning-relevant body measurements of children and youth

A = Height
B = Eye level
C = Upward reach
D = Forward reach
E = Upper body height when seated
F = Seat height
G = Eye level when seated
H = Seat depth
I = Seat width

Figure 2.2 Dimensions (in cm) of people performing various activities

Age	3	5	7	9	11	13	15	16–17	18–19
Height	93–111	106–126	118–138	127–148	134–160	149–173	155–183	155–188	156–189
Forward reach	39–48	41–53	46–58	52–64	55–69	61–75	62–77	62–79	62–79
Upward reach	105–127	122–144	134–159	151–179	159–192	173–210	178–219	181–219	187–226
Eye level	85–99	96–112	106–127	117–137	125–149	138–164	145–172	145–174	145–175
Upper body height when seated	53–62	57–70	64–75	67–78	70–82	74–92	81–94	83–97	83–98
Eye level when seated	42–52	47–57	51–63	57–70	59–75	63–79	69–84	70–86	71–86
Seat height	19–28	25–32	28–35	30–38	34–41	36–45	39–49	39–50	39–50
Seat depth	23–29	26–36	30–40	35–43	40–47	40–49	43–54	44–54	44–55
Seat width	25–35	27–37	29–39	31–41	32–43	33–43	33–44	34–45	37–48

	Men				Women			
Age	18–25	26–40	41–60	61–65	18–25	26–40	41–60	61–65
Height	168.5–179.0	166.5–176.5	163.0–183.5	160.5–180.5	156.0–176.0	154.5–172.5	161.5–170.5	151.0–168.5
Forward reach	70.0–82.5	68.5–82.0	68.0–81.0	67.5–80.0	63.5–76.0	63.0–75.0	62.0–74.5	61.5–74.0
Upward reach	200.0–224.5	199.0–222.0	196.0–219.5	193.0–215.0	185.5–208.5	184.5–203.5	183.5–200.5	182.0–195.5
Eye level	156.5–178.5	154.5–175.0	151.0–172.0	149.0–169.0	145.0–164.5	144.0–161.5	142.0–159.0	139.5–157.0
Upper body height when seated	87.5–98.5	86.5–97.5	84.5–96.0	83.0–94.5	83.0–93.0	82.0–91.5	80.5–90.5	79.0–90.0
Eye level when seated	76.0–87.0	74.5–86.0	73.0–85.0	71.0–83.0	72.0–82.0	71.0–81.0	70.0–80.0	68.5–79.5

Table 2.1 Planning-relevant body measurements of children, youth, and adults (in cm) as a function of age

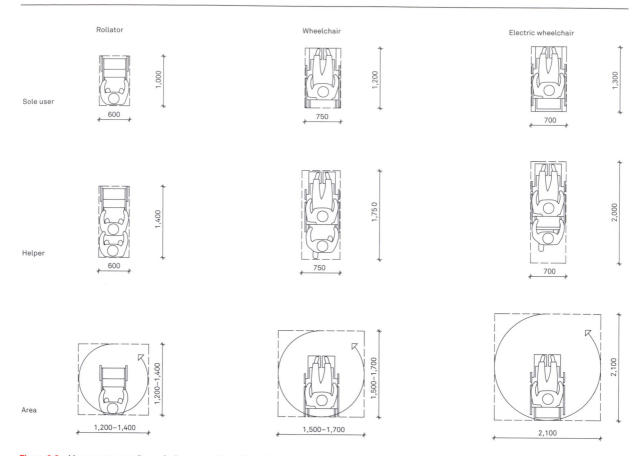

	Rollator	Wheelchair	Electric wheelchair

Figure 2.3 Movement areas (in mm) of people with walking aids or wheelchairs

Since electrically powered wheelchairs mostly tend to be used outdoors, areas of sufficient size must be provided there to ensure their barrier-free use. However, this also applies to interior entrance areas because changes between wheelchairs ordinarily take place inside the building.

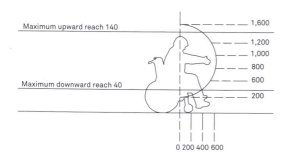

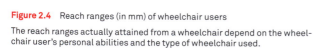

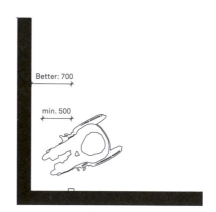

Figure 2.4 Reach ranges (in mm) of wheelchair users

The reach ranges actually attained from a wheelchair depend on the wheelchair user's personal abilities and the type of wheelchair used.

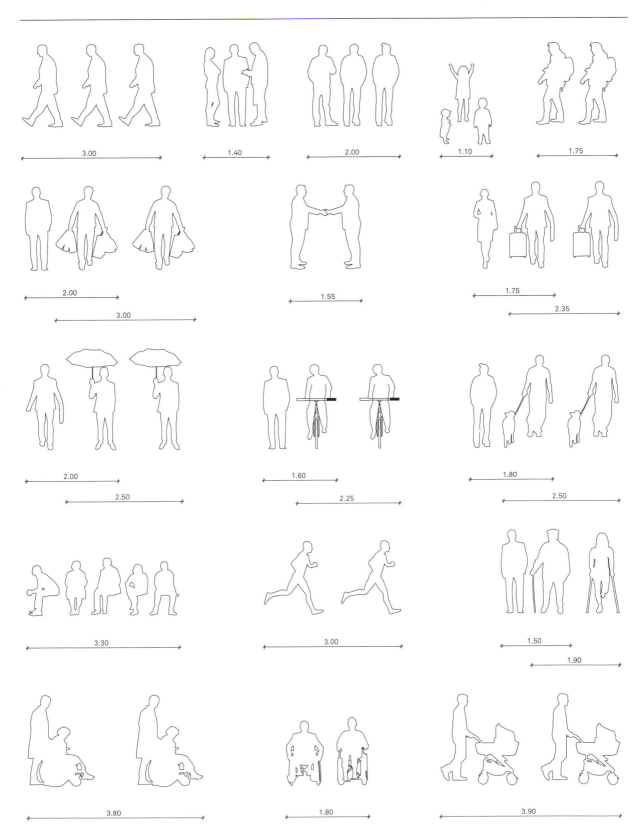

Figure 2.5 Area requirements (in m) for groups of people

3.00

1.40

2.00

1.10

1.75

2.00

3.00

1.55

1.75

2.35

2.00

2.50

1.60

2.25

1.80

2.50

3.30

3.00

1.50

1.90

3.80

1.80

3.90

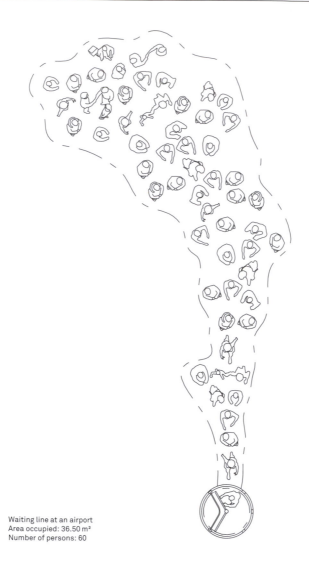

Waiting line at an airport
Area occupied: 36.50 m²
Number of persons: 60

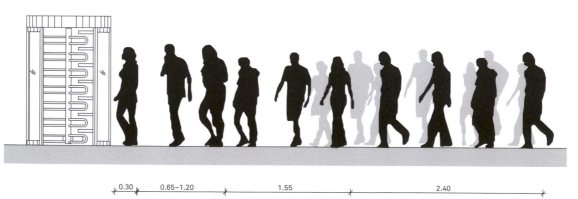

0.30   0.65–1.20   1.55   2.40

Example of a waiting line (in m)

Figure 2.6   Area requirements for waiting lines

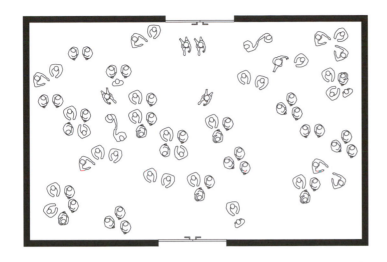

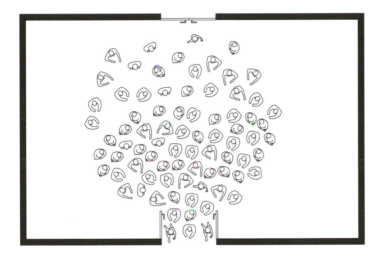

Area of room: approx. 100 m²
Number of persons: 81

Figure 2.7 Area requirements for human crowds

3 Outdoor Spaces

Infrastructure development for buildings encompasses diverse measures in the public realm and in ensuring access and supply logistics on the property. In addition to roads, bicycle paths, and walkways, this includes access restrictions such as perimeter enclosures, gates, etc., and built elements located on the property (waste container areas, lighting, doorbells, mailboxes, etc.). The connections to public utility services (such as electricity, water supply, sewer, etc.) are also to be planned in this context.

3.1 Street Spaces and Vehicles

Public spaces and infrastructures are to be designed with attention to aspects of accessibility and are fundamental to the participation of as many people as possible in public life and activities relating to mobility. Thus it is of little help to design a building according to current requirements for accessibility if disabled persons cannot reach it independently via public access routes.

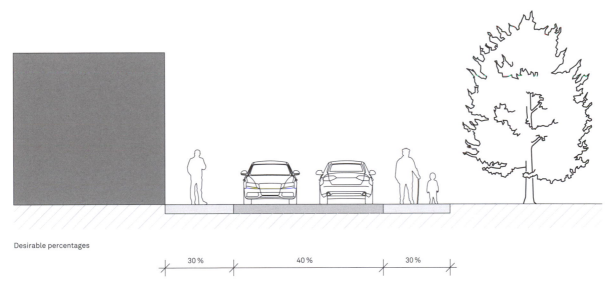

Desirable percentages

30 %   40 %   30 %

Figure 3.1 Sensible allocation of street spaces

Street space widths						
Use	Residential lane	Residential street	Collector road	Neighborhood street	Rural main road	Local thoroughfare
Without public transit	4.50–10.00 m	9.00–17.00 m	11.50–15.50 m	12.00–17.50 m	8.50–14.00 m	
With public transit bus service		11.00–16.50 m	16.50–26.70 m	16.50–21.50 m	11.50–19.50 m	12.50–21.20 m
Use	Local shopping street	Main shopping street	Commercial street	Industrial road	Connecting road	Non-built-up road
With public transit bus service	20.50–30.20 m	20.50–33.00 m	16.50–38.00 m	23.50–30.00 m	19.70–31.45 m	15.50–28.60 m
With tram	24.20–34.20 m	16.50–37.00 m	16.50–38.00 m		19.70–39.70 m	28.50–34.10 m

Table 3.1 Typical widths of street spaces

Widths of street spaces vary depending on traffic volume (vehicles/hr.)
Author's summary, based on RASt 06

Element	Space required
Advisory bike lane for cyclists on the roadway	0.50–1.50 m
Areas for children to play by the roadside	2.00 m
Areas in front of benches	1.00 m
Areas in front of shop displays	1.50 m
Bikeway	1.60–2.50 m
Bus lane	3.25 m
Curb strip (road verge) with trees	2.00–2.50 m
Curb strip (road verge) without trees	1.00 m
Median	1.00–2.50 m
Parallel parking	2.30–2.50 m
Parking, delivery, loading	2.50–3.00 m
Pedestrian and cycle path	3.00–5.00 m
Perpendicular parking	5.00–5.50 m
Roadside area with frontage road	7.00–7.50 m
Spaces for lingering in front of store windows	1.00 m
Sidewalk	2.25–7.00 m
Waiting areas at bus stops	2.50 m

Table 3.2 Typical widths of elements along roadways

Distance	Safety clearance
From buildings, boundary enclosures, tree pits, traffic facilities, and other built-in elements	0.25 m
From edge of roadway	0.50 m
From parked vehicles (parallel parking)	0.75 m
From parked vehicles (perpendicular or angled parking)	0.25 m
From pedestrian traffic areas	0.25 m

Table 3.3 Safety clearances for cycling facilities

Type of restriction or assistive equipment	Width	Length
Blind person with white cane	0.80–1.20 m	–
Blind person with guide dog	1.20 m	–
Blind person with escort	1.10–1.30 m	–
Person with baby carriage	0.80–1.00 m	2.00 m
Person with cane	0.85 m	–
Person with crutches	1.00 m	–
Person in wheelchair	0.90–1.10 m	–
Wheelchair user with escort	0.90–1.00 m	2.50 m

Table 3.4 Space required for barrier-free access

Vehicle category	Example		Length	Width	Diameter of turning circle	Turning radius
Subcompact car			3.50 m	1.65 m	9.60 m	4.80 m
Compact car			4.00 m	1.70 m	10.60 m	5.30 m
Mid-sized car			4.40 m	1.80 m	11.00 m	5.50 m
Mid-luxury car			4.80 m	1.85 m	11.50 m	5.75 m
Luxury car			5.00 m	1.95 m	11.90 m	5.95 m

Table 3.5   Dimensions of miscellaneous vehicles

Type	Example		Length	Width	Height
Bicycle			1.70–2.00 m	0.60–0.75 m	1.00–1.25 m
Motorcycle			2.00–2.50 m	0.70–1.00 m	1.00–1.50 m
Quad bike			1.75–2.10 m	1.05–1.25 m	1.00–1.25 m

Table 3.6   Dimensions of trucks

Type	Number of persons*	Dimensions*			Turning circle*	Turning curve*
	Seated/standing	Length	Width	Height	Diameter	Radius
Public transit bus						
Low-floor bus, city bus	30–55 / 75–110	12.00–18.00 m	2.50–2.55 m	3.00–3.30 m	21.00–23.00 m	10.50–11.50 m
Regional bus	40–60 / 20–70	12.00–18.00 m	2.50–2.55 m	3.15–3.40 m	21.00–23.00 m	10.50–11.50 m
Minibus	10–20 / 12–30	5.90–9.00 m	1.95–2.15 m	2.60–2.90 m	13.50–17.50 m	6.75–8.75 m
Minivan	< 9	4.75–5.30 m	1.90–2.00 m	1.90–2.50 m	11.50–13.80 m	5.75–6.90 m
Double-decker bus	50–90 / 10–45	13.00–14.00 m	2.50–2.55 m	3.90–4.00 m	22.00–24.00 m	11.00–12.00 m
Articulated bus	35–60 / 80–150	17.50–19.50 m	2.50–2.55 m	3.00–3.30 m	22.50–24.50 m	11.25–12.25 m
Bi-articulated bus	45–60 / < 150	23.50–25.00 m	2.50–2.55 m	3.00–3.30 m	22.50–25.00 m	11.25–12.50 m
Intercity bus (coach)						
Intercity bus with toilet	40–60	12.00–14.50 m	2.50–2.55 m	3.30–3.75 m	20.50–24.00 m	10.25–12.00 m
Sleeper bus ("Nightliner")	6–12	12.00–14.00 m	2.50–2.55 m	3.70–4.00 m	20.50–24.00 m	10.50–12.00 m

Table 3.7 Dimensions of buses

* Average dimensions based on manufacturers' data

Permissible total weight	Length	Width	Height
max. 3.5 t	5.25–7.45 m	2.40–2.45 m	2.45–3.10 m
max. 7.5 t	6.00–8.50 m	2.45–2.55 m	3.80 m
max. 12 t	6.50–12.00 m	2.45–2.55 m	3.80–4.00 m
40 t	13.50–18.75 m	2.55 m	3.80–4.00 m
Truck, 2 axles	max. 13.50 m	max. 2.55 m	max. 4.00 m
Truck, min. 3 axles	max. 15.00 m	max. 2.55 m	max. 4.00 m
Tractor-trailer	max. 16.50 m	max. 2.55 m	max. 4.00 m
Truck-trailer combination	max. 18.75 m	max. 2.55 m	max. 4.00 m

Table 3.8 Dimensions of trucks

3.1 Street Spaces and Vehicles

Minimum space required by delivery vehicles	Width	Length
Delivery vans and small trucks	2.30 m	10.00–12.00 m
Large trucks	2.50 m	12.00–14.00 m
Tractor-trailers	2.50 m	16.50 m
Temporary storage areas for goods	3–5 m²	

Table 3.9 Area requirements for loading and delivery

Type	Length	Width	Height	Turning radius
Backhoe loader	3.40–6.75 m	1.40–2.35 m	2.25–3.10 m	4.00–6.50 m
Concrete mixer	8.00–15.00 m	2.50–2.55 m	3.80–4.00 m	
Concrete pump	8.00–15.00 m	2.50–2.55 m	3.80–4.00 m	
Crawler excavator	9.10–14.00 m	2.50–4.85 m	3.00–4.10 m	
Mobile crane	10.00–22.00 m	2.55–3.00 m	3.55–4.00 m (25.00–145.00 m)	
Mini-excavator	3.25–5.50 m	0.95–2.30 m	2.25–2.95 m	
Self-propelled excavator	6.25–10.25 m	2.50–2.75 m	3.10–3.25 m	4.50–6.65 m
Wheeled front loader	5.30–10.00 m	2.30–2.75 m	2.75–3.65 m	3.50–7.00 m
Bulldozer	4.00–7.65 m	2.35–3.00 m	3.10–4.00 m	

Table 3.10 Dimensions of construction vehicles

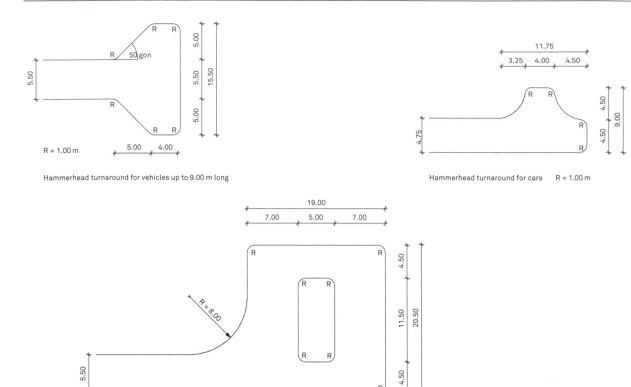

Hammerhead turnaround for vehicles up to 9.00 m long

R = 1.00 m

Hammerhead turnaround for cars   R = 1.00 m

Hammerhead turnaround for 3-axle vehicles   R = 1.00 m

Figure 3.2   Hammerhead turnarounds for cars

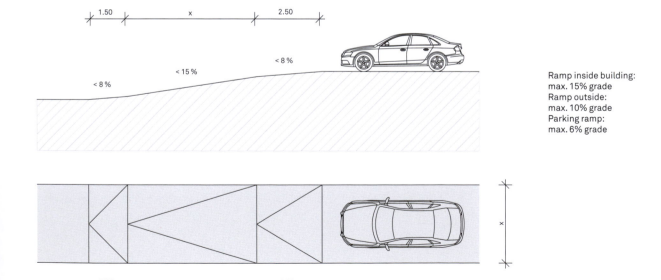

Ramp inside building:
max. 15% grade
Ramp outside:
max. 10% grade
Parking ramp:
max. 6% grade

Figure 3.3   Design of ramps and ramp transitions for motor vehicles

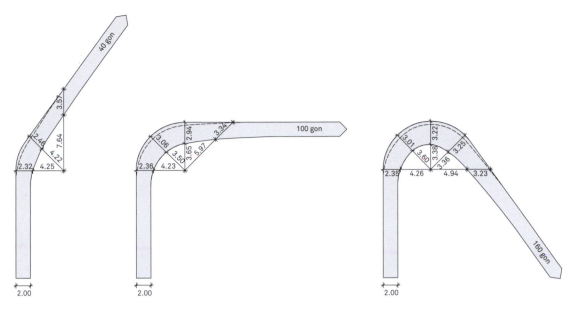

Figure 3.4 Turning curves for cars

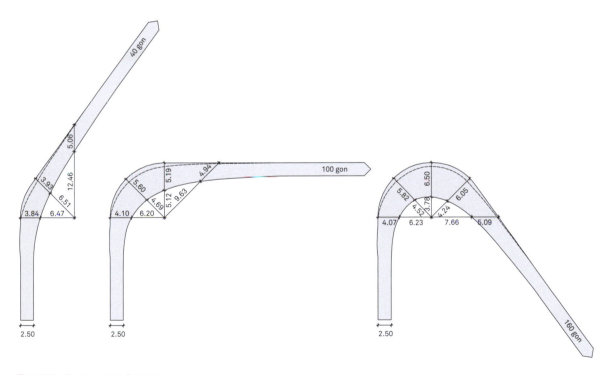

Figure 3.5 Turning curves for trucks

3.2 Parking Spaces

Parking spaces for cars, bicycles, buses, and/or trucks are an important factor for planning, since they occupy large amounts of exterior space. For all parking spaces, consideration must be given to ensure good vehicular accessibility and ease of entering, exiting, and loading the vehicle.

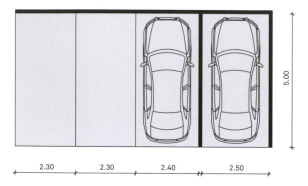

Minimum dimensions:
2.50 m when confined on both sides
2.40 m when confined on one side
2.30 m when open on both sides
For comfortable use, parking spaces should always have a width of at least 2.50 m so that car doors can be opened approximately 45°.

Figure 3.6 Dimensions of parking spaces for passenger cars

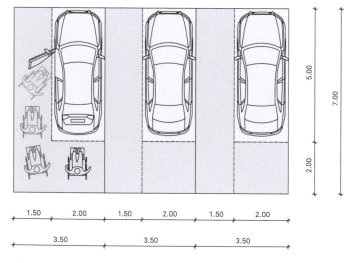

It is important to ensure that a wheelchair-accessible transition is established between the maneuvering zone and the walkway.

Figure 3.7 Dimensions of wheelchair-accessible parking spaces

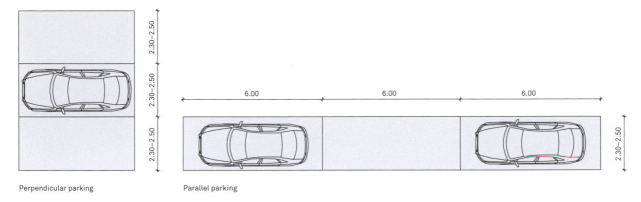

Perpendicular parking

Parallel parking

Figure 3.8 Parking variants and dimensions

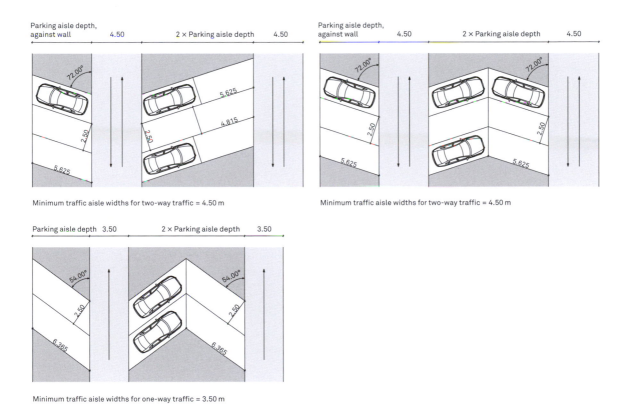

Minimum traffic aisle widths for two-way traffic = 4.50 m

Minimum traffic aisle widths for two-way traffic = 4.50 m

Minimum traffic aisle widths for one-way traffic = 3.50 m

Figure 3.9 Parking variants and dimensions

Parking angle [gon]	Parking angle [°]	Parking aisle depth, against wall [m]	Parking aisle depth, bumper-to-bumper interlock [m]
50	45	4.85	8.25
60	54	5.15	9.00
70	63	5.30	9.60
80	72	5.35	9.90
90	81	5.25	10.00

Table 3.11 Parking aisle depth as a function of parking angle

Type	Length	Width	Height
Single carport	5.00–8.00 m	2.90–3.80 m	2.10–3.10 m
Double carport	5.00–8.00 m	5.00–6.00 m	2.10–3.10 m
Single-car garage	5.10–9.00 m	2.55–4.00 m	2.20–3.50 m
Double-car garage	5.10–9.00 m	5.00–8.00 m	2.20–3.50 m

Table 3.12 Typical carport and garage sizes

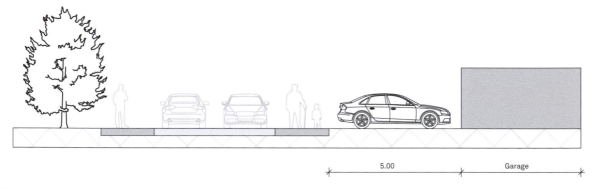

5.00   Garage

Figure 3.10 Minimum space between garage and road

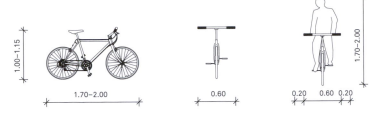

Figure 3.11   Bicycle dimensions

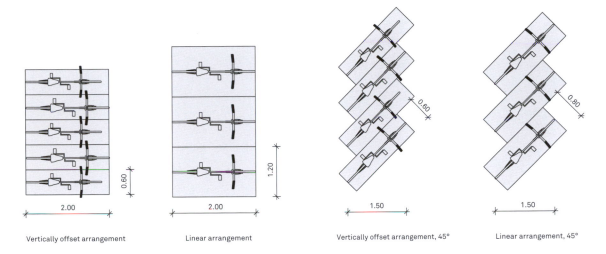

Vertically offset arrangement

Linear arrangement

Vertically offset arrangement, 45°

Linear arrangement, 45°

Figure 3.12   Parking spaces for bicycles

Arrangement	Width in m	Length in m
Parking space, linear	1.20	2.00
Parking space, vertically offset	0.60	2.00
Parking space (45°), linear	0.80	1.50
Parking space (45°), vertically offset	0.60	1.50
Parking space, rack (narrow spacing)	0.80	2.00
Parking space, rack (comfortable spacing)	1.20	2.00
Parking space, rack, vertically offset (narrow)	1.00	2.00
Parking space, rack, vertically offset (comfortable)	1.20	2.00
Bike box	1.00	2.10

Table 3.13   Dimensions of bicycle parking spaces

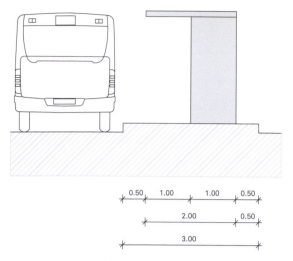

Figure 3.13 Bus stop platform with waiting area/waiting island

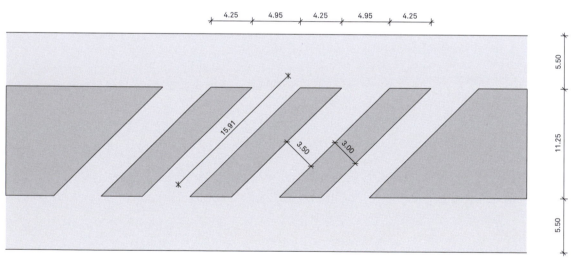

Figure 3.14 Bus parking lot with passenger islands

3.2 Parking Spaces

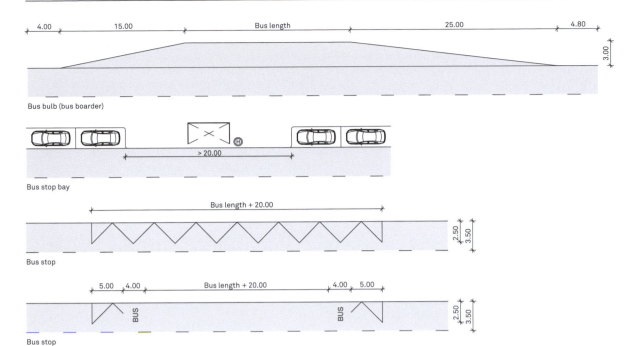

Bus bulb (bus boarder)

Bus stop bay

Bus stop

Bus stop

Figure 3.15 Various types of bus stops

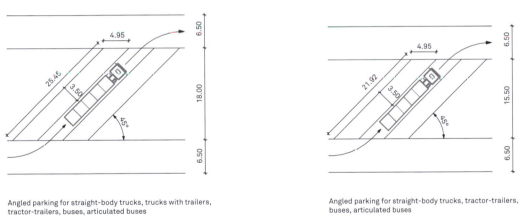

Angled parking for straight-body trucks, trucks with trailers,
tractor-trailers, buses, articulated buses

Angled parking for straight-body trucks, tractor-trailers,
buses, articulated buses

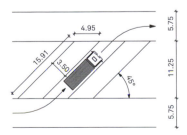

Angled parking for straight-body trucks, 12 m buses

Figure 3.16 Angled parking for straight-body trucks, trucks with trailers,
tractor-trailers, buses, articulated buses

3.3 Private Exterior Circulation

In exterior areas, various built elements are also used for diverse purposes, which include controlling access to the property, facilitating circulation and logistics on the property, and making a transition to the building. For their design and configuration, the degree of public or private exposure and the security requirements appropriate to the building typology are usually crucial.

Typical exterior built elements:
- Entrances such as gates, barriers, doors, etc.
- Physical access control using electronic systems or gates with security guards
- Fences, walls
- Lighting
- Mailboxes
- Waste receptacles and enclosures
- Playgrounds, benches
- etc.

Doorbell and mailbox units represent an interface between public and private space, since they should be publicly accessible and the mailboxes should, where possible, be capable of being emptied directly from the private realm. Mailbox units can be located outside the building as free-standing elements, on or in the exterior wall, or in the entry area.

For aesthetic reasons and to reduce offending odors, areas for the disposal of waste are located apart from the building and preferably shielded from view. When planning these areas, however, it is important to bear in mind that the containers must be easily and directly accessible for the building's occupants and collection vehicles alike. In general, the sizes of waste receptacles used in any one locality are standardized, so enclosures can be planned accordingly. For the sake of accessibility, different height levels are desirable so as to ensure that the openings for disposal are also within reach of wheelchair users.

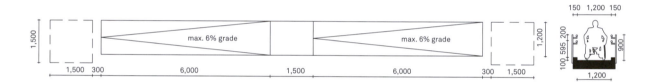

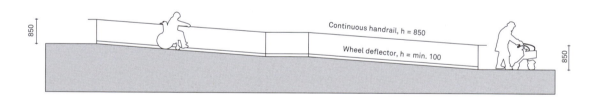

Figure 3.17   Ramps and passing areas for wheelchair users
The specified requirements also pertain to ramps within buildings.

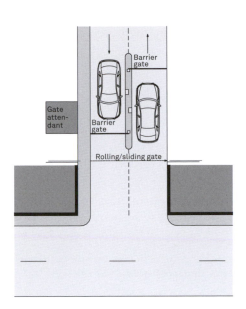
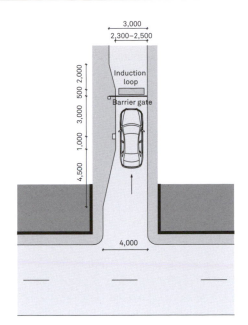

Figure 3.18 Access control with barrier gates

Security revolving door

Full-height security turnstile

Full-height turnstile

Exact dimensions vary by manufacturer, so the specified dimensions can only serve as guidelines.
CH = Clear passage height
FH = Fascia height
OH = Overall height

Figure 3.19 Various access control systems

Dimensions for mail slots of mailboxes			
Size	Height of mail slot	Length of mail slot	Compatible letter formats (max.)
1	30–35 mm (Type 4 up to 40 mm, as long as the space between the bottom of the mail slot and the bottom of the box at the removal side is at least 680 mm)	325–400 mm	Max. B4 inserted lengthwise, E4 and C3 inserted sideways
2	30–35 mm (Type 4 up to 40 mm, as long as the space between the bottom of the mail slot and the bottom of the box at the removal side is at least 680 mm)	230–280 mm	Max. B4 inserted lengthwise, C4 inserted sideways
3 (only types 1–3)	35–45 mm	325–400 mm	Max. B4 inserted lengthwise, E4 and C3 inserted sideways

Table 3.14 Dimensions of mail slots

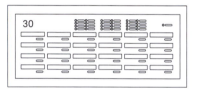

Figure 3.20 Integration of doorbell/mailbox units within wall cladding

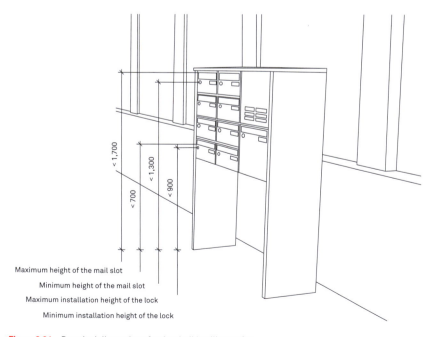

Figure 3.21 Practical dimensions for doorbell/mailbox units

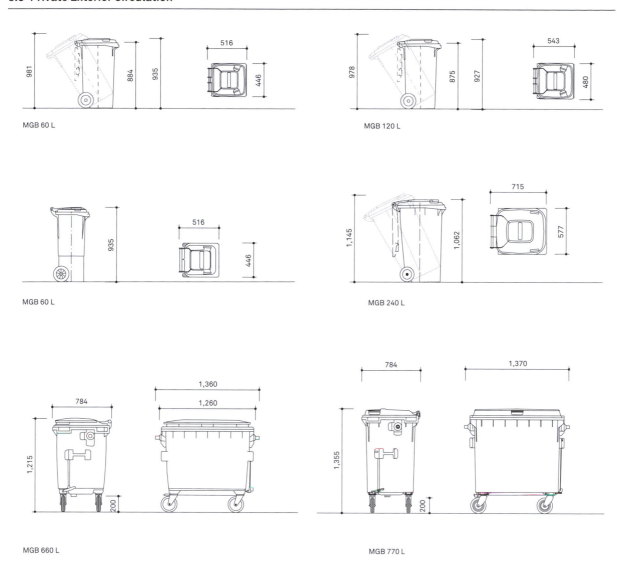

MGB 60 L

MGB 120 L

MGB 60 L

MGB 240 L

MGB 660 L

MGB 770 L

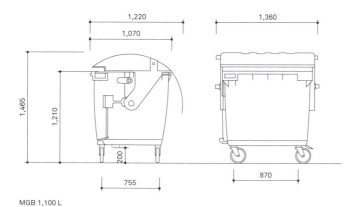

MGB 1,100 L

Figure 3.22 Common waste container sizes, in mm

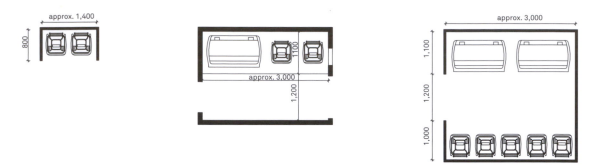

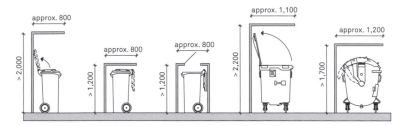

Figure 3.23 Dimensions of waste collection rooms and enclosures

In building classes 3 to 5, the walls, ceilings, and interior doors of waste collection rooms must have a suitable fire rating. They require constant ventilation and should be capable of being emptied directly from outside the building.

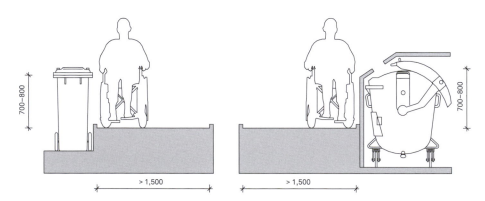

Figure 3.24 Accessibility of waste receptacles for wheelchair users

3.3 Private Exterior Circulation

Symmetrical containers with a capacity of 2–4 m³ and a maximum width of 1,520 mm for skip loader vehicles

Asymmetrical containers with a capacity of 3–5 m³ and a maximum width of 1,520 mm for skip loader vehicles

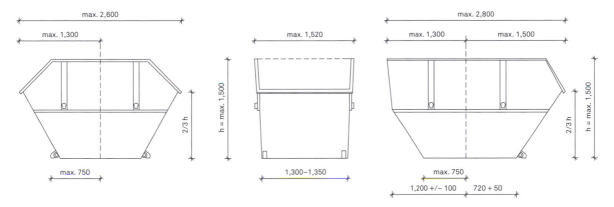

Figure 3.25 Dimensions of containers of various capacities

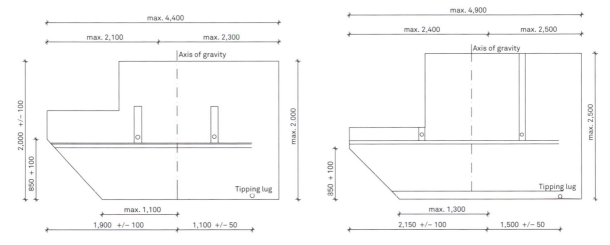

Figure 3.26 Exemplary dimensions of trash compactors

Trash compactors are available in many shapes and sizes that are dependent on the waste products to be processed and the desired result. Thus consideration must be given to the specific requirements and the manufacturer's product data.

4 Circulation Spaces

Building entrances are ordinarily approached from the public realm via a pedestrian path. But depending on the building typology and logistical needs, a means of access must also be considered for cars, trucks, buses, bicycles, walking aids, wheelchairs, baby carriages, etc. Especially for typologies that are heavily frequented at peak periods (theaters, sports facilities, nursery schools, etc.), suitably effective concepts are needed to accommodate the very high frequencies encountered there briefly. This also includes temporary or long-term parking of vehicles and equipment in private outdoor spaces or buildings.

Buildings should generally be approachable via accessible ramps and paths. Thus any difference in height between street level and the top of the finished floor at the entrance level, which may not be excessive, should receive attention. The internal circulation of a building ordinarily consists of elements such as entrance areas, corridors, doors, stairs, elevators, etc. Depending on whether a building is public or private, the entrance areas can be designed with open plans and integrated vertical circulation or organized instead in a more functional, spatially efficient, and expedient manner. Of equal importance is whether the internal circulation serves different functional units or solely acts as a distributor within a single functional unit.

4.1 Entrance Areas

Entrance areas fulfill a variety of tasks pertaining to functions that include communication, access, security, and supervision. The entrance area gives people a first impression, making it the "calling card" of the building. Because they convey initial intuitive information about the building's users (companies or individuals), entrance areas have a very strong psychological impact. Moreover, entrance areas are thermal and acoustic buffer zones. In the case of fire, they serve as an escape route, and for people with disabilities they represent a crucial link between the public realm and functions inside the building.

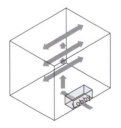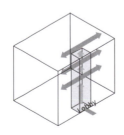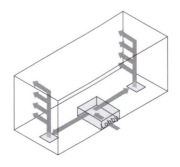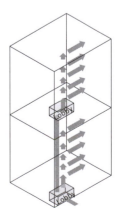

Figure 4.1   Organization of entrance areas and internal circulation

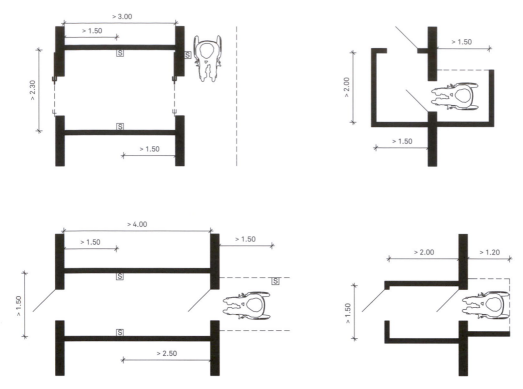

Figure 4.2 Dimensions of wheelchair-accessible vestibules

Automatic door opener controls must be positioned for operation within reach of wheelchair users, and they should be located at least 1.50 m away from doors (2.00 m from doors swinging toward user).

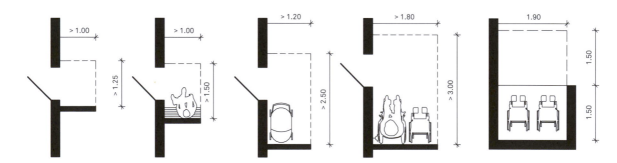

Figure 4.3 Space requirements for private entrance areas

It is important to create sufficient storage space for baby carriages and strollers, wheelchairs, bicycles, etc., in the entrance area to ensure uninterrupted free movement between inside and outside, depending on the typology.

4.2 Corridors

In addition to providing access, corridors can serve as communication areas as well as zones for waiting, resting, or encounters. Depending on the type of use, measures for improving qualities that create a pleasant atmosphere in those spaces, such as natural lighting and views to the exterior, should therefore also be considered.

For escape and rescue routes, specific requirements are placed on the clear widths of corridors, the elimination of smoke and fire loads, the surrounding building components, and the paths and doors leading to the exterior. To this end, fire compartmentation in buildings is also essential.

For designing accessible corridors, further measures are also needed in addition to providing sufficient widths for wheelchair users. The elderly and people with impaired mobility require handrails and opportunities to sit at short intervals. Using high-contrast colors on doors, frames, floors, etc. helps by providing guidance to the visually impaired.

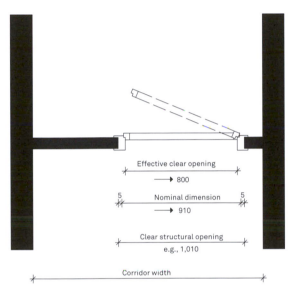

Figure 4.4   Definition of the various opening widths

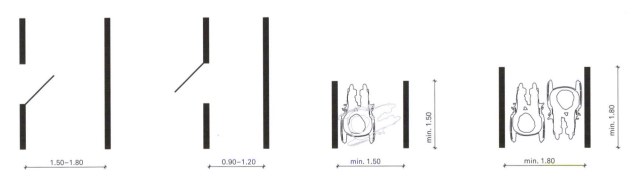

Figure 4.5   Minimum widths of corridors as a function of door swing direction

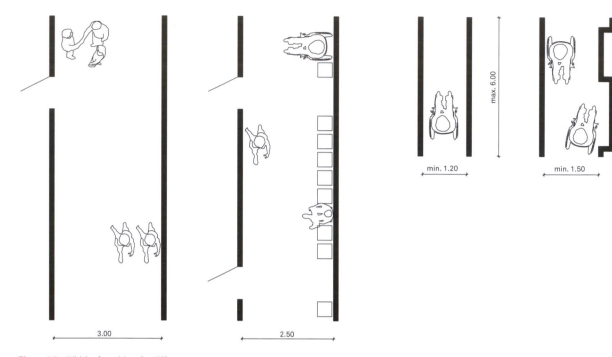

Figure 4.6   Width of corridors for different uses

Escape route length	Clear ceiling height
≤ 30.00 m	≤ 5.00 m
≤ 35.00 m	> 5 ≤ 7.50 m
≤ 40.00 m	> 7.50 ≤ 10.00 m
≤ 45.00 m	> 10.00 m ≤ 12.50 m
≤ 50.00 m	> 12.50 ≤ 15.00 m
≤ 55.00 m	> 15.00 ≤ 17.50 m
≤ 60.00 m	> 17.50 m

Table 4.1   Escape route length as a function of the clear ceiling height in places of assembly

An escape route length of 30 m may not be exceeded unless it is compensated by corresponding room height.
As per MVStättV

Circulation path	Clear width
Minimum width of circulation paths according to number of persons served	
max. 5 people	0.875 m
max. 20 people	1.00 m
max. 200 people	1.20 m
max. 300 people	1.80 m
max. 400 people	2.40 m
At doors, a reduction to the minimum width of corridors can be disregarded if the constriction is not more than 0.15 m. Regardless, the clear width may not be less than 0.80 m at any point.	
Aisles to personally assigned workstations, auxiliary stairs	0.60 m
Maintenance aisles, aisles to infrequently used operating equipment	0.50 m
Pedestrian routes between storage facilities and equipment	1.25 m
Pedestrian routes in secondary corridors of storage facilities, used exclusively for loading and unloading by hand	0.75 m
Circulation paths between rail vehicles with speeds of ≤ 30 km/h and without permanent fixtures in the circulation paths	1.00 m
Maneuvering paths	1.30 m

Table 4.2   Minimum widths of paths for pedestrian traffic
As per ASR A1.8

Room	Maximum length
In ordinary workspaces	35.00 m
Areas with high fire risk, equipped with automatic fire extinguishing devices	35.00 m
Areas with high fire risk, not equipped with automatic fire extinguishing devices	25.00 m
Areas endangered by toxic substances and/or explosion	20.00 m
Areas endangered by explosive materials	10.00 m

Table 4.3   Maximum escape route length in workplaces
As per ASR A2.3

4.3 Doors

As connecting elements between rooms or maneuvering zones, doors are an important design element. Doors are subject to specific requirements, especially along escape and rescue routes and at wheelchair-accessible entrances. As potential bottlenecks, doors play a central role in maintaining the necessary clear width of an escape route and hence they can also determine the necessary corridor width.

For many doors, the direction of swing is often dictated by the function. For instance, all escape and rescue path doors must, as a basic rule, open in the direction of the escape route. Individual room doors that adjoin an escape and rescue path can ordinarily be oriented inward as desired.

Door type	Barrier-free	Escape and rescue path	Fire protection
Hinged door	x	x	x
Sliding door	x		
Folding door	x		
Swing door	x		
Revolving door			
Automatic door	x	(x)	(x)

Table 4.4 Range of applications for various door types

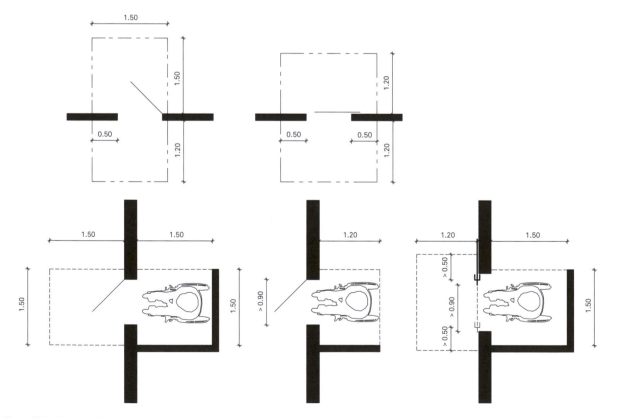

Figure 4.7 Minimum dimensions for wheelchair maneuvering areas at door

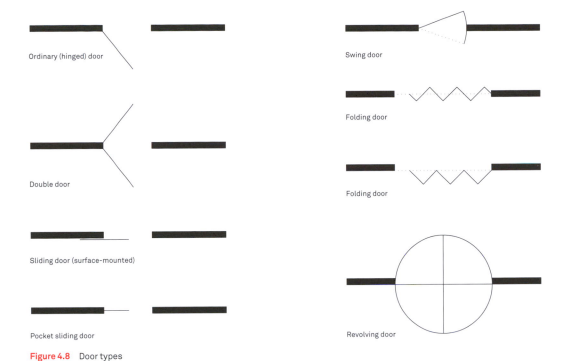

Figure 4.8   Door types

Ordinary (hinged) door

Double door

Sliding door (surface-mounted)

Pocket sliding door

Swing door

Folding door

Folding door

Revolving door

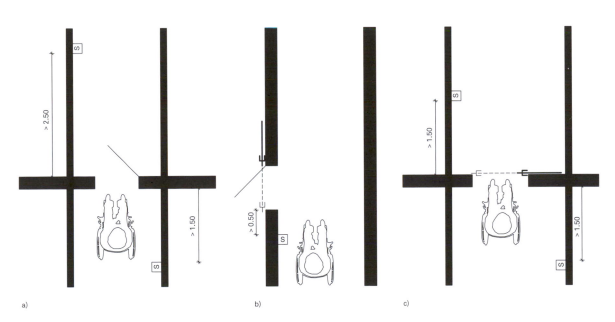

a)   b)   c)

Figure 4.9   Requirements for the placement of automatic door openers

a) Distance between activation button and hinged door with frontal approach
b) Distance between activation button and hinged or sliding door with side approach
c) Distance between activation button and sliding door with frontal approach

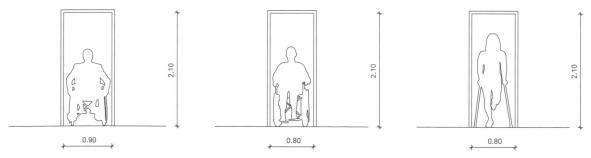

Figure 4.10 Minimum widths for use of wheelchairs or walking aid

2-leaf revolving door

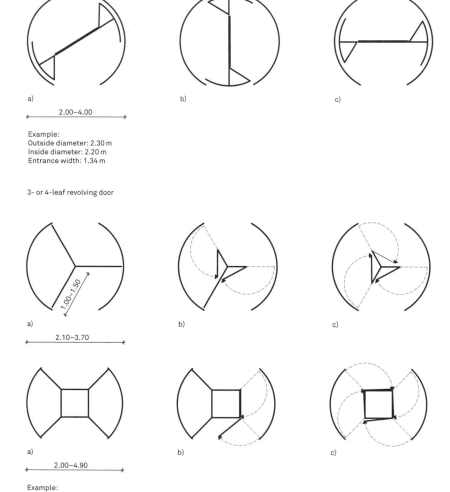

a)   b)   c)   d)

2.00–4.00

Example:
Outside diameter: 2.30 m
Inside diameter: 2.20 m
Entrance width: 1.34 m

3- or 4-leaf revolving door

a)
1.00–1.50
2.10–3.70

b)   c)

a)
2.00–4.90

b)   c)

Example:
Outside diameter: 2.30 m
Inside diameter: 2.20 m
Entrance width: 1.474 m

Above:
a) Basic position
b) Night closure
c) Middle position "Night/bank function," closure with controlled entry through additional sliding door
d) Middle position with open sliding door (Emergency egress position)

Below:
a) Basic position
b) Escape opening
c) Free passage

Figure 4.11 Various revolving door types

4.4 Stairs

Stairs and stair enclosures serve as escape and rescue routes and as functional or communicative links between different stories or levels.

The geometry and minimum dimensions of a stair are dependent on the type of use, the number of people who might need to flee in an emergency, and the desired ease of use. It is generally very important to identify the number of risers and the geometry of the stairway early on in the design process.

For designing and dimensioning stairs, the following rules apply (r = riser, t = tread):

- Stride length rule: t + 2r = 630 mm (+/− 30 mm)
- Safety rule: t + r = 460 mm (+/− 10 mm)
- Comfort rule: t − r = approx. 120 mm

An intermediate landing must be provided after no more than 18 steps. For determining stair widths, the free escape route width as well as handrails or guardrails and any stairwell openings must be taken into account. Stair railings must be designed so there is neither a risk of injury to children (max. 120 mm gaps) nor a possibility of climbing over the railing.

To enable barrier-free use of the stairs by the visually impaired, highly visible markings and Braille numbering on the handrail are desirable. Similarly, a high-contrast design of the landings and the top and bottom steps is helpful.

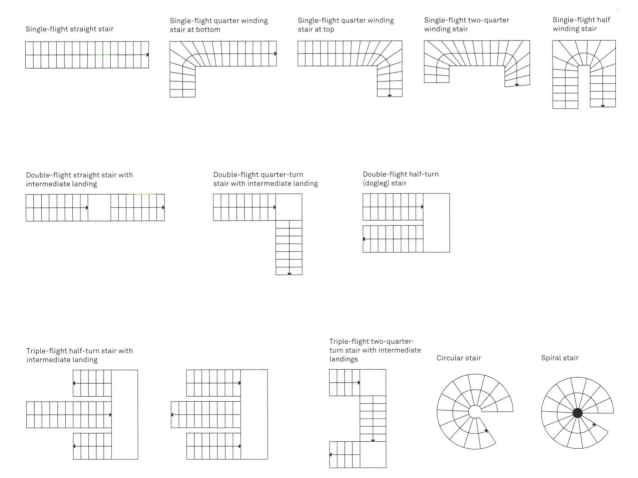

Single-flight straight stair

Single-flight quarter winding stair at bottom

Single-flight quarter winding stair at top

Single-flight two-quarter winding stair

Single-flight half winding stair

Double-flight straight stair with intermediate landing

Double-flight quarter-turn stair with intermediate landing

Double-flight half-turn (dogleg) stair

Triple-flight half-turn stair with intermediate landing

Triple-flight two-quarter-turn stair with intermediate landings

Circular stair

Spiral stair

Figure 4.12 Typical stair geometries

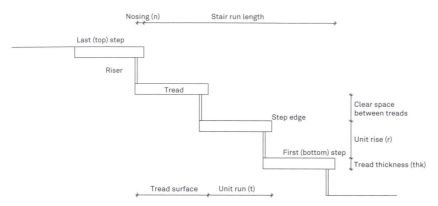

Figure 4.13 Terminology for stairs

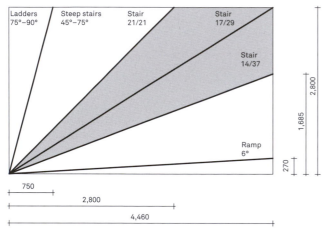

Figure 4.14 Stair types according to rise-to-run ratio

Construction type	Unit run (t)	Unit rise (r)
Exterior stairs, child day care facilities	320–300 mm	140–160 mm
Places of assembly, administrative buildings for public bodies, schools, after school centers	310–290 mm	150–170 mm
Commercial buildings, miscellaneous buildings	300–260 mm	160–190 mm
Auxiliary stairs	300–210 mm	140–210 mm

Table 4.5 Requirements for stair risers and treads
As per ASR A1.8

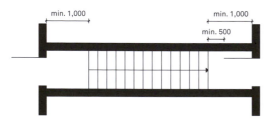

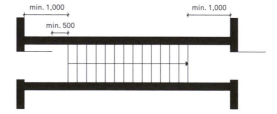

Figure 4.15 Clearance between doors and stairs

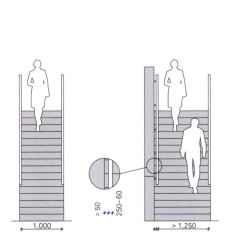

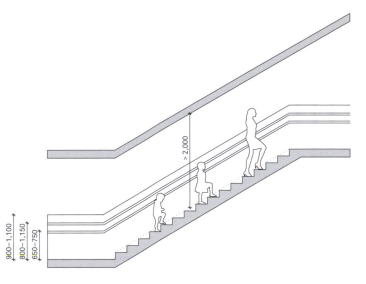
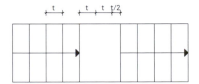

Figure 4.16   Determining the clear dimensions of stairs

For simultaneous use by multiple people, the clear stair width should be at least 1.25 m.

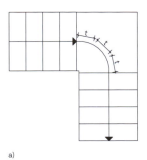

a)

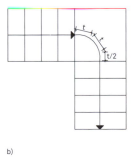

b)

Figure 4.17   Minimum size of landings

A landing is needed after max. 18 risers
a) Typical buildings
b) Residential buildings with max. 2 apartments

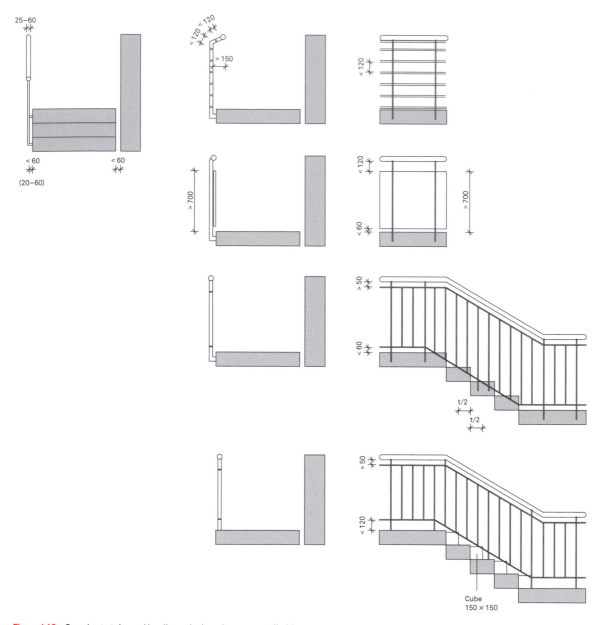

Figure 4.18   Guards at stairs and landings, designed to prevent climbing

Floor-to-floor height in m	Riser/tread ratio (r/t) in mm					
	165/300	170/290	175/280	180/270	185/260	Optimum riser/tread ratio
2.80	17 × r/t = **5.10** (2.80)	16 × r/t = **4.64** (2.72)	16 × r/t = **4.48** (2.80)	15 × r/t = **4.20** (2.70)	15 × r/t = **3.90** (2.77)	**17 × 165 / 300 = 5.10**
3.00	18 × r/t = **5.40** (2.97)	18 × r/t = **5.22** (3.06)	17 × r/t = **4.76** (2.97)	17 × r/t = **4.59** (3.06)	16 × r/t = **4.16** (2.96)	**17 × 176 / 277 = 4.70**
3.20	19 × r/t = **5.70** (3.13)	19 × r/t = **5.51** (3.23)	18 × r/t = **5.04** (3.15)	18 × r/t = **4.86** (3.24)	17 × r/t = **4.42** (3.14)	**18 × 177 / 276 = 4.96**
3.40	20 × r/t = **6.00** (3.30)	20 × r/t = **5.80** (3.40)	19 × r/t = **5.32** (3.32)	19 × r/t = **5.13** (3.42)	18 × r/t = **4.68** (3.33)	**19 × 179 / 272 = 5.16**
3.60	22 × r/t = **6.60** (3.63)	21 × r/t = **6.09** (3.57)	20 × r/t = **5.60** (3.50)	20 × r/t = **5.40** (3.60)	19 × r/t = **4.94** (3.51)	**20 × 180 / 270 = 5.40**
3.80	23 × r/t = **6.90** (3.79)	22 × r/t = **6.38** (3.74)	22 × r/t = **6.16** (3.85)	21 × r/t = **5.67** (3.78)	20 × r/t = **5.20** (3.70)	**22 × 173 / 284 = 6.24**
4.00	24 × r/t = **7.20** (3.96)	23 × r/t = **6.67** (3.91)	23 × r/t = **6.44** (4.02)	22 × r/t = **5.94** (3.96)	22 × r/t = **5.72** (4.07)	**23 × 174 / 282 = 6.48**

Table 4.6   Rough guidelines for total runs (lengths) of stairs (in m)
Riser/tread ratios calculated according to stride length rule
2r + t = 630 mm (+/− 30 mm)

Escape route width in m	0.875	1	1.2	1.25	1.5	1.8	2
Single-flight stair	0.975−1.025	1.10−1.15	1.30−1.35	1.35−1.40	1.60−1.65	1.90−1.95	2.10−2.15
Double-flight stair	2.00−2.10	2.25−2.35	2.65−2.75	2.75−2.85	3.25−3.35	3.85−3.95	4.25−4.35

Table 4.7   Rough guidelines for stairway widths
Varies as a function of one-/two-sided handrail and open well at double-flight stairs

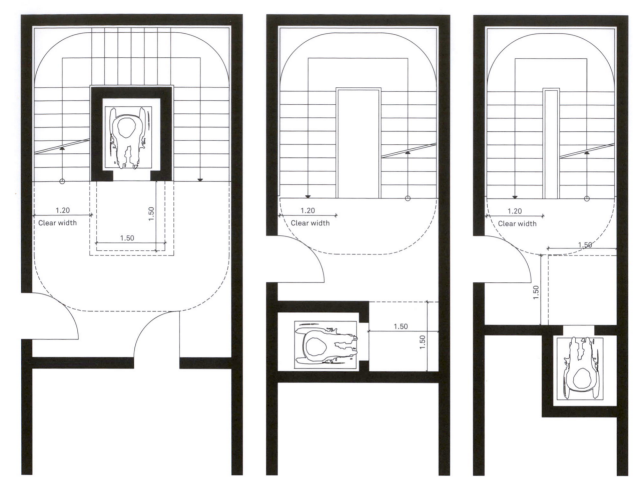

Figure 4.19 Clear escape route widths in stairways

4.5 Ramps

Ramps represent a good option for bridging small height differences, such as in entrance zones. Ramps that should also be accessible for wheelchair use are subject to specific requirements. They are permitted to have a maximum grade of 6 percent and must be provided with rest plat-

forms after no more than 4 m. In addition to the technical requirements pertaining to widths, lengths, wheel rails, etc., the areas at the ends of the ramp should be sensibly designed to minimize safety hazards.

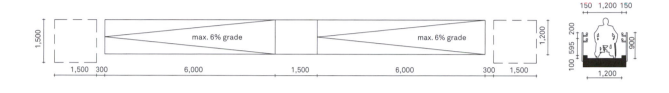

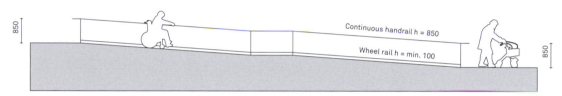

Figure 4.20 Technical requirements for accessible ramps

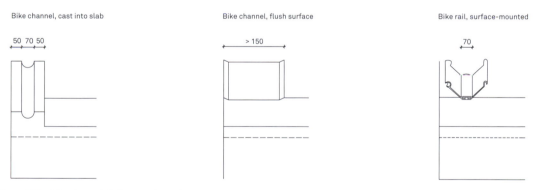

Figure 4.21 Bike channels/rails on stairs and ramps

4.6 Escalators and Moving Walkways

Escalators ensure speedy transport of larger numbers of people between different floor levels. They must be designed for a maximum inclination of 30–35° and their points of connection to the structure must be dimensioned according to the manufacturer's specifications. Depending on whether they are used simultaneously by standing and walking persons, the step width is between 600 and 1,000 mm. Moving walkways can also be used as inclined planes (moving ramps) that accommodate shopping carts or the like. Moving walkways with little or no inclination are used as passenger conveyors for bridging longer distances, such as in airports or shopping malls.

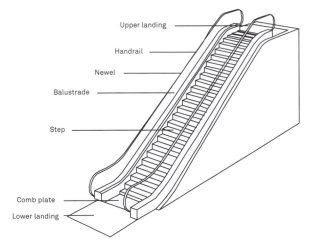

Figure 4.22 Components of escalators

Upper landing
Handrail
Newel
Balustrade
Step
Comb plate
Lower landing

Floor-to-floor height (H)	Overall length of escalator (30° incline) L = H × 1.732 + 4,731	Overall length of escalator (35° incline) L = H × 1.428 + 4,825
3,000	9,927	9,109
3,500	10,793	9,823
4,000	11,659	10,537
4,500	12,525	11,251
5,000	13,391	11,965
5,500	14,257	12,679
6,000	15,123	13,393

Overall length of the escalator

Table 4.8 Overall lengths of escalators for installation (in mm)

The length and width of the openings vary by manufacturer. These are standard dimensions given here only for general orientation.

4.6 Escalators and Moving Walkways

Escalators

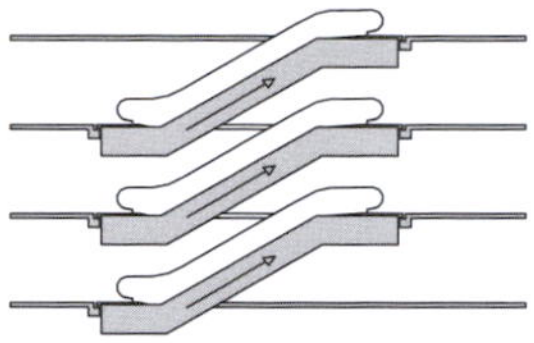

Parallel layout of escalators

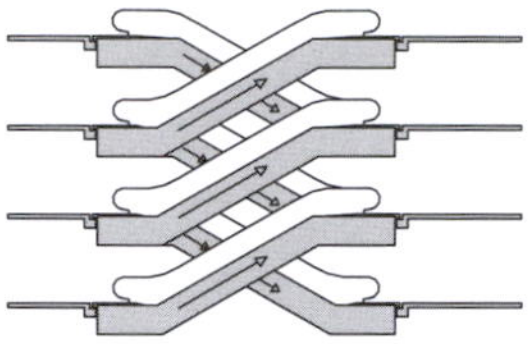

Crisscross layout of escalators

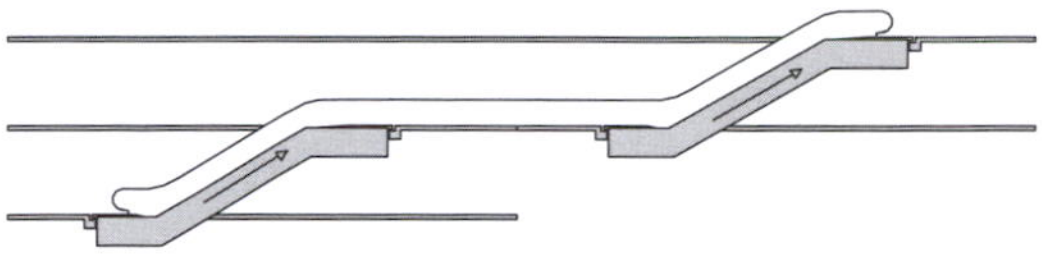

Sequential escalators

Moving ramps

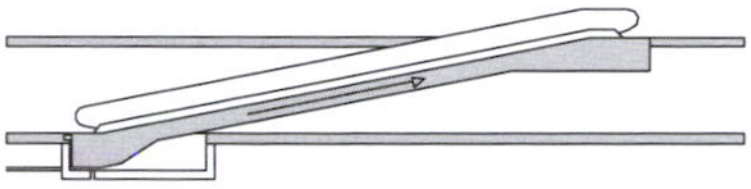

Single

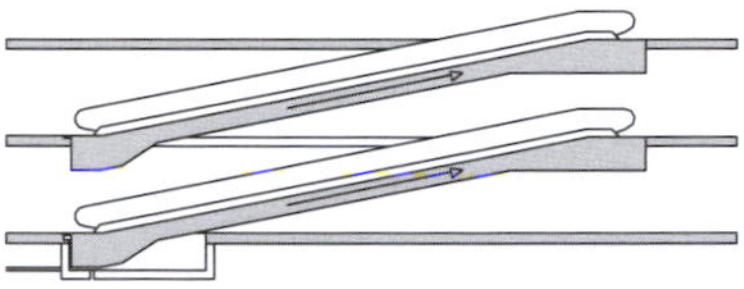

Double

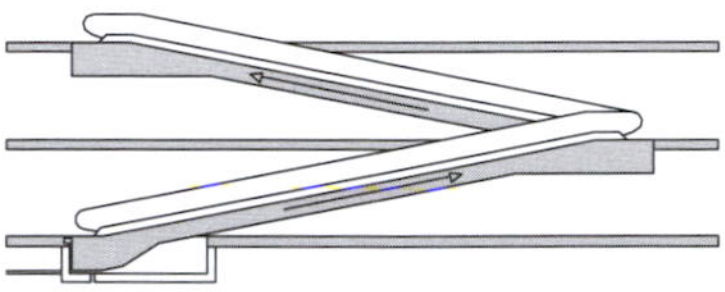

Scissor layout

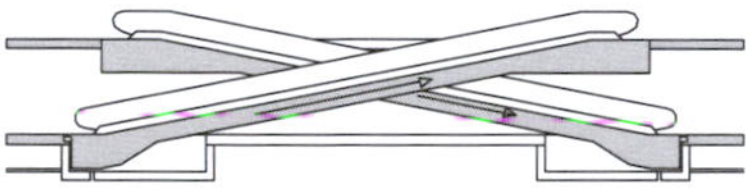

Crisscross layout

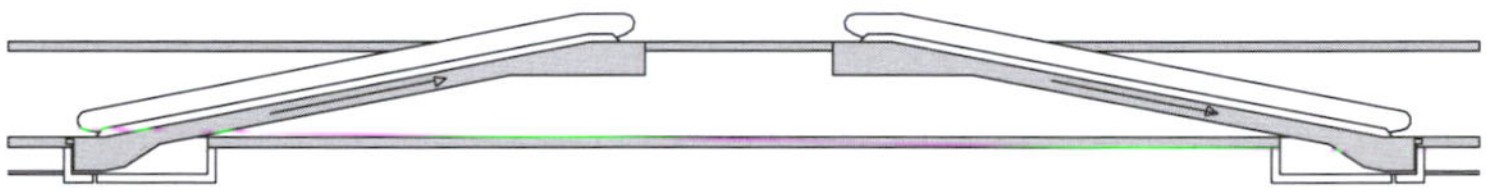

Opposing directions

Figure 4.23 Vertical circulation with escalators/moving ramps

Circulation with escalators must be dimensioned according to the anticipated number of visitors.
For relevant circulation paths, such as in train stations, the width should be dimensioned so that both standing and walking persons can use the escalator at the same time.

Inclination of escalator	Max. travel height in mm	Width of step in mm	Length of the opening in level I in mm	Length of the opening at level II and above in mm	Width of the opening in mm
30°	6,000	600/800/1,000	4,450	Min. 6,476	1,200/1,400/1,600
30°	8,000	600/800/1,000	4,850	Min. 6,876	1,200/1,400/1,600
30°	6,500/13,000	800/1,000	4,850	Min. 7,003	1,400/1,600
35°	6,000	600/800/1,000	4,250	Min. 5,837	1,200/1,400/1,600

Table 4.9 Floor opening sizes for the installation of escalators

The length and width of the openings vary by manufacturer. These are standard dimensions given here only for general orientation.

Escalator

Plan

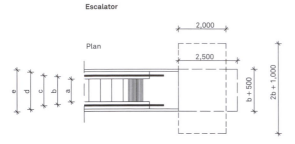

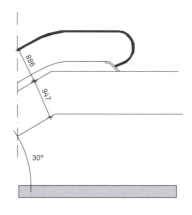

	in mm	in mm	in mm
a: Step width	600	800	1,000
b: Width between handrails	758	958	1,158
c: Handrail center spacing	838	1,038	1,238
d: Escalator width	1,140	1,340	1,540
e: Width of pit	1,200	1,400	1,600

Connection points
Elevation

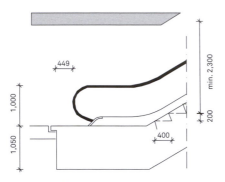

Figure 4.24 Dimensions of escalators

Moving walkway

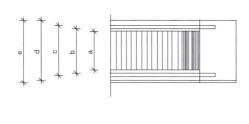

	in mm	in mm
a: Pallet width	800	1,000
b: Width between handrails	958	1,158
c: Handrail center spacing	1,038	1,238
d: Moving walkway width	1,340	1,540
e: Width of pit	1,400	1,600

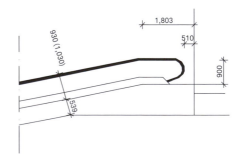

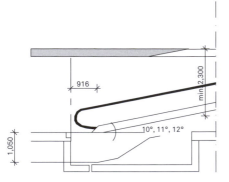

Figure 4.25 Dimensions of moving walkways

4.7 Elevators and Conveying Systems

Elevators transport people and freight between stories or different levels of a building. A distinction is made between passenger elevators, service elevators (carries passengers and goods), and freight elevators (no passengers). Passenger elevators are essential for barrier-free circulation in multistory public buildings, but they are also requisite in residential buildings without barrier-free requirements if there are five or more stories. Especially when adapting existing buildings, smaller lifting platforms are often used to overcome small changes in height in order to make the building accessible to wheelchair users. In high-rise buildings, large numbers of users usually necessitate complex control systems that can enable the use of multiple cars in a single shaft, automatically manage available cars with destination selection control, or serve distribution levels with dedicated express elevators.

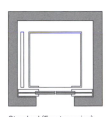
Standard (Front opening)

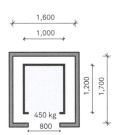
Front and rear opening

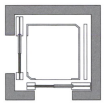
Front and side opening

Figure 4.26   Elevator door openings

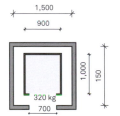
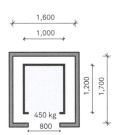
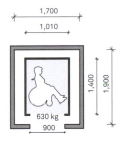
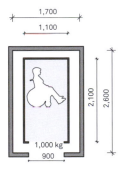

Figure 4.27   Passenger elevators for residential buildings

Elevator type	Number of persons	Nominal loading (kg)	Car width (CW)	Car depth (CD)	Door width (DW)	Hoistway width (HW)	Hoistway depth (HD)		Door rough opening (DRO)
							Door one-sided	Doors on opposite sides	
					Standard sizes – all dimensions in mm				
Passenger elevators	3	240	700	900	600	1,170	1,280	–	900
	4	320	900	1,000	700	1,370	1,450	–	1,000
			750	1,100	700	1,300	1,500	–	1,000
	5	400	800	1,200	700	1,300	1,600	1,810	1,000
		400	950	1,100	700	1,420	1,500	1,710	1,000
					800	1,450	1,500	1,710	1,100
	6	450	1,000	1,200	800	1,470	1,600	1,810	1,100
					900	1,600	1,600	1,810	1,200
		480	950	1,300	700	1,420	1,700	1,910	1,000
					800	1,450	1,700	1,910	1,100
					900	1,600	1,700	1,910	1,200
			1,000	1,250	800	1,470	1,650	1,860	1,100
					900	1,600	1,650	1,860	1,200
Barrier-free	8	630	1,100	1,400	800*	1,800	1,700	1,810	950
					900	2,000	1,700	1,810	1,050
	10	800	1,350	1,400	800*	1,900	1,800	–	950
					900	2,000	1,800	–	1,050
	12	900	1,400	1,500	800*	1,950	1,850	1,910	950
					900	2,000	1,850	1,910	1,050
	13	1,000	1,100	2,100	800*	1,800	2,400	2,510	950
					900	2,000	2,400	2,510	1,050
					1,000	2,200	2,400	2,510	1,150
			1,600	1,400	900	2,150	1,850	–	1,050
					1,000	2,200	1,850	–	1,150
					1,100	2,400	1,850	–	1,250

* 900 mm door width required under German law

Table 4.10 Dimensions of elevators

Elevator type	Number of persons	Nom- inal loading (kg)	Car width (CW)	Car depth (CD)	Door width (DW)	Hoistway width (HW)	Hoistway depth (HD)		Door rough opening (DRO)
							Door one-sided	Doors on opposite sides	
					Standard sizes – all dimensions in mm				
	15	1,150	1,200	2,100	800*	1,800	2,400	2,510	950
					900	2,000	2,400	2,510	1,050
					1,000	2,200	2,400	2,510	1,150
			1,600	1,550	900	2,150	1,850	–	1,050
					1,000	2,200	1,850	–	1,150
					1,100	2,400	1,850	–	1,250
Hospital bed elevators for nominal loading of 1,275 kg or greater	17	1,275	2,000	1,400	1,100	2,700	2,000	–	1,250
	21	1,600	2,100	1,600	1,100	2,800	2,100	–	1,250
			1,400	2,400	1,300	2,300	2,850	–	1,450
				2,300	1,300	2,300	2,750	2,990	1,450
	24	1,800	2,350	1,600	1,200	3,050	2,100	–	1,350
	26	2,000	2,350	1,700	1,200	3,050	2,150	–	1,350
			1,500	2,600	1,300	2,350	3,050	3,290	1,450
				2,700	1,300	2,350	3,150	–	1,450

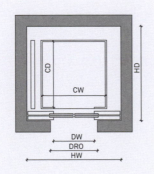
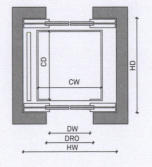

* 900 mm door width required under German law

Table 4.10 (continuation)   Dimensions of elevators

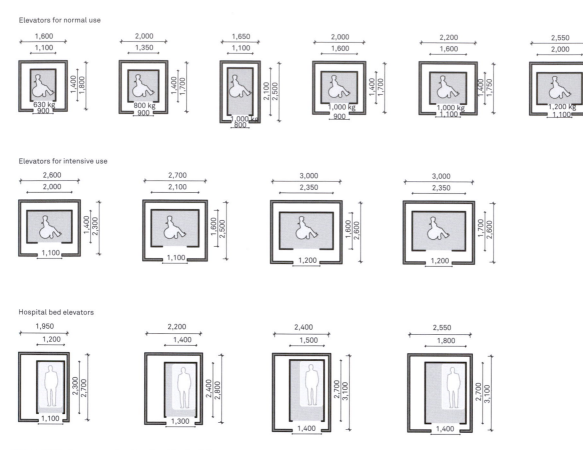

Figure 4.28   Passenger elevators for other buildings

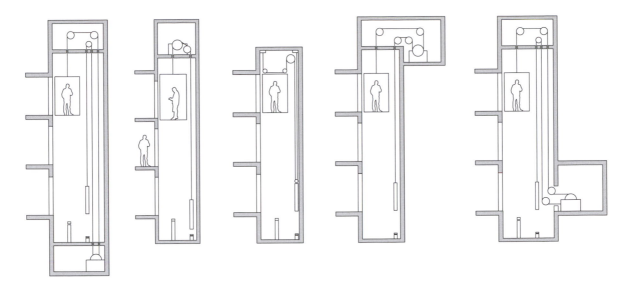

Figure 4.29 Location of elevator machinery (rooms)

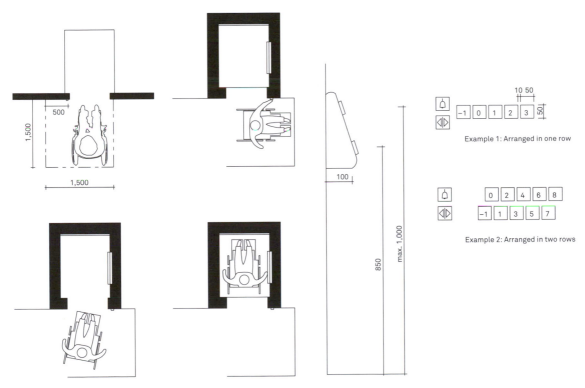

Figure 4.30 Use of elevators with a wheelchair

Example 1: Arranged in one row

Example 2: Arranged in two rows

Figure 4.31 Accessible elevator operating controls

5 Living and Sleeping Spaces

Spaces for living and sleeping must meet a multitude of demands, as they can have a major influence on the inhabitants' private daily rhythm and cadence of life. As varied as people's needs, living concepts, and phases of life are, their living environment must accordingly be designed heterogeneously. The spectrum extends from classic residential layouts, in which each individual function – such as sleeping, cooking, etc. – is assigned a specific room, to completely open living landscapes and shared space concepts. Living rooms and bedrooms are sometimes tailored precisely to their users, allowing them to be designed in a highly individual manner. For rental housing, by contrast, the living rooms and bedrooms are subject to generally applicable standards so as to ensure that the apartment is appealing for future tenants, who may frequently change. The same applies to hotel rooms, which are equipped and furnished according to general standards and categories defined by the hotel industry.

Due to the diversity of possibilities, this chapter deals primarily with typical furnishings.

5.1 Living Spaces

Living rooms and shared spaces offer places of retreat, are used to pursue leisure activities within the house, and serve as settings to receive guests. By using large French doors, living spaces with direct access to a garden or balcony can be extended outdoors. The degree to which living spaces are designed to be extroverted or introverted depends heavily on each individual's personal needs.

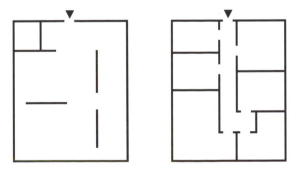

Figure 5.1 Open layout of housing unit (left) with flowing transitions between rooms; detailed cellular layout (right) with central corridor circulation system

Room	1–4 persons	Each additional person
Living room with dining area	18–20 m²	+ 2 m²
Living room without dining area	18 m²	+ 2 m²
Bedroom, 1 bed	8 m²	
Bedroom, 2 beds	12 m²	
Storage space	2% of habitable area (minimum 1 m²)	

Table 5.1 Minimum requirements for room sizes

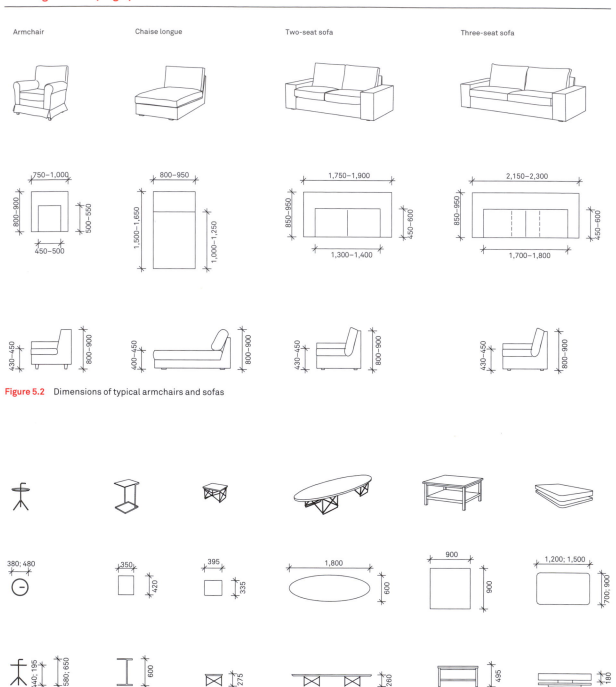

Figure 5.2 Dimensions of typical armchairs and sofas

Figure 5.3 Dimensions of typical couch and side tables

5.2 Bedrooms

The position of bedrooms within an apartment should be remote from potential sources of noise, and away from the street. Within a residential unit, it is common to arrange several bedrooms in the direct proximity of a shared bathroom. Individual en suite bathrooms are another option, and common in some countries.

In bedrooms for adults it may be necessary to provide larger areas to accommodate a baby cot, changing table, or other equipment.

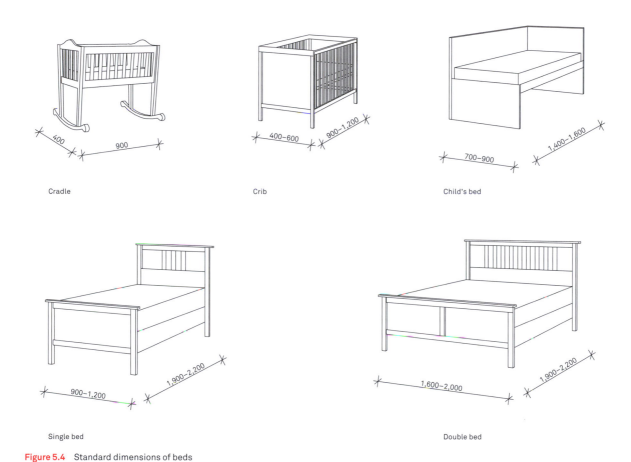

Cradle

Crib

Child's bed

Single bed

Double bed

Figure 5.4   Standard dimensions of beds

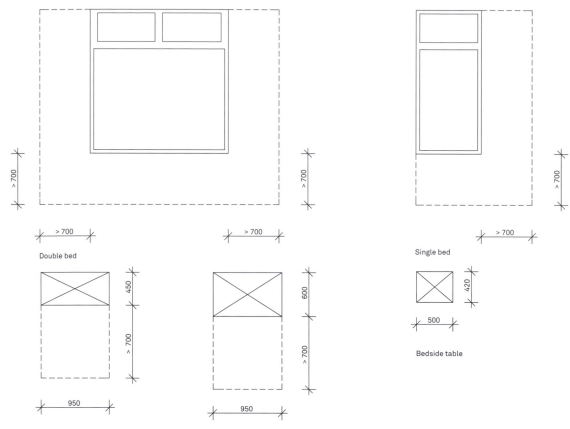

Double bed

Single bed

Bedside table

Figure 5.5 Furniture and movement space in the bedroom

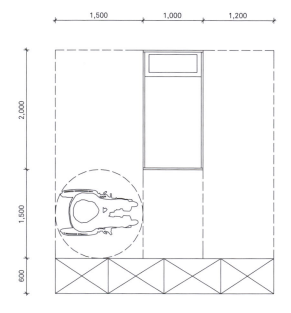

In a barrier-free bed arrangement, the two long sides of the bed should be kept clear and there should be adequate distance to furniture and adjoining walls. This guarantees that the bed is accessible to wheelchair users and care personnel in sheltered accommodation.

Figure 5.6 Barrier-free bed arrangement

5.3 Hotel Rooms

The design of hotel rooms is largely determined by the level of comfort provided, which has to comply with the intended star category of the hotel. The range of rooms is considerable and varies significantly in type, fit-out, and size. Types of rooms are:

- Single room
- Double room
- Twin-bed room
- Multiple-bed room
- Family room
- Dormitory
- Junior suite
- Suite
- Apartment
- Studio
- Interconnected rooms
- Duplex/maisonette

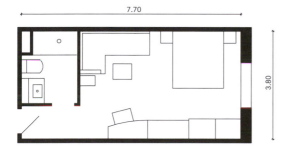 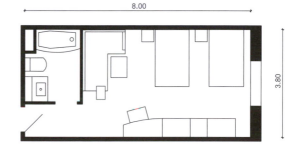

Figure 5.7   Sample layouts
Left: King standard USA; right: Double twin standard EU

EU		USA		UK	
Designation	Size in cm	Designation	Size in cm	Designation	Size in cm
Small Single	80 × 200	–	–	Small Single	75 × 191
Single	90 × 200	Single/Twin	97 × 191	Single	91 × 191
Large Single	100 × 200	Extra-long twin	100 × 203	Super Single	107 × 191
–	–	–	–	Small Double	120 × 198
Double	140 × 200	Double/Full	137 × 191	Double	137 × 198
King	160 × 200	Queen	152 × 203	King	152 × 198
Super King	180 × 200	King	193 × 203	Super King	183 × 198
–	–	California King	180 × 213	–	–

Table 5.2   Bed sizes and designations

6 Kitchen and Dining Areas

The preparation of food and beverages embraces a broad spectrum, from kitchenettes in private apartments, hotel rooms, or offices to professional commercial kitchens. Even though kitchen areas are often designed on a very individual basis, there are established geometric and hygienic requirements that must be adhered to as minimum standards. As soon as a kitchen is used commercially, local requirements of the authorities for trade supervision and sanitary inspection must be observed in addition.

6.1 Kitchen Fixtures and Appliances

For residential use, most kitchen fixtures and appliances (such as cabinets, stoves, ovens, refrigerator/freezers) are available with a depth of approximately 60–65 cm and a standard nominal width of 60 cm, which are complemented by additional unit spacings of 30 cm, 45 cm, 90 cm, 120 cm, etc. for cabinetry and other furnishings. In the food and beverage industry, additional sizes are also encountered, which are partly based on modular Gastro-Norm food containers and partly on the size of technical equipment.

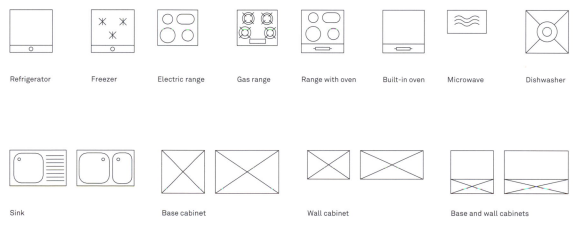

| Refrigerator | Freezer | Electric range | Gas range | Range with oven | Built-in oven | Microwave | Dishwasher |

| Sink | Base cabinet | Wall cabinet | Base and wall cabinets |

Figure 6.1   Drawing symbols for various kitchen elements

Minimum widths for sinks
a) Individual sink unit
b) Sink unit with 1½ bowls
c) Double bowl sink unit without drainboard
d) Double bowl sink unit with drainboard

Examples of various shapes and
sizes of sinks

Examples of
a) Glass ceramic/induction cooktops
b) Gas cooktops

Cooktops with special shapes
a) Kidney-shaped
b) Fan-shaped
c) Oval cooktop

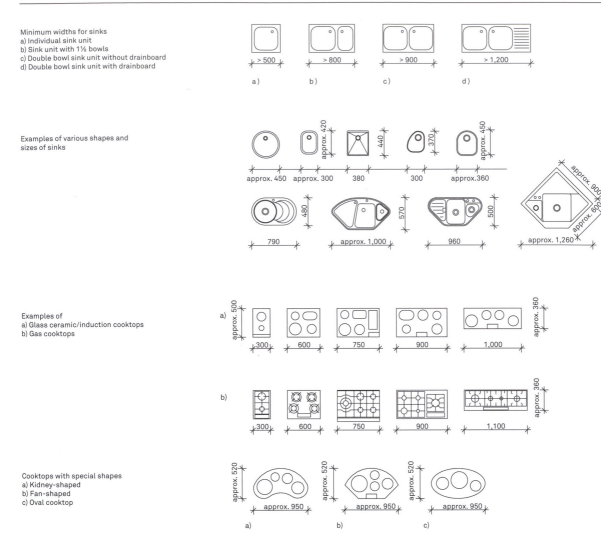

Figure 6.2   Typical dimensions for sinks and cooktops

Required minimum clearances in kitchens in mm	
Distance between two opposite kitchen counter units (storage surfaces)	1,200
Distance between kitchen counter unit and opposite wall	1,200
Distance between two opposite kitchen counter units, wheelchair-accessible	1,500
Distance between kitchen counter unit and opposite wall, wheelchair-accessible	1,500
Gaps between kitchen counter unit and adjacent walls	30
Distance between kitchen counter unit and door/window frames	100

Table 6.1   Minimum clearances in kitchen areas

6.1 Kitchen Fixtures and Appliances

Plan dimensions of food service containers

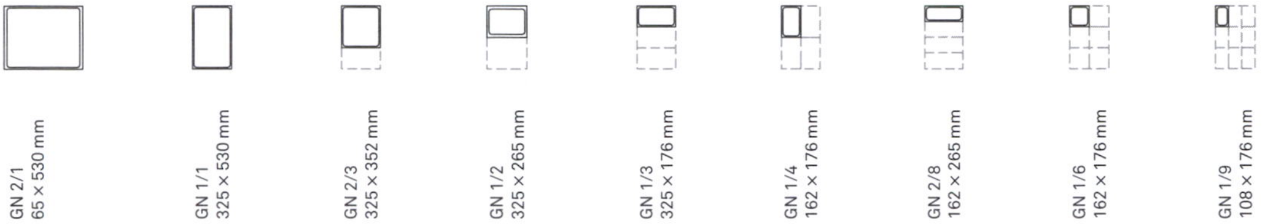

| GN 2/1 65 × 530 mm | GN 1/1 325 × 530 mm | GN 2/3 325 × 352 mm | GN 1/2 325 × 265 mm | GN 1/3 325 × 176 mm | GN 1/4 162 × 176 mm | GN 2/8 162 × 265 mm | GN 1/6 162 × 176 mm | GN 1/9 108 × 176 mm |

Deep fryer with
2 10-liter tanks

Bain-marie

Electric cooktop
with 4 cooking
elements

Griddle with
splash guards
at the sides

Commercial kettle
Ø 400 mm

Sink unit

Examples of commercial kitchen appliances with dimensions of 700 × 700 × 850 mm (w × d × h).
Other widths (400, 500, 600, 800, 900 mm) and depths (600, 650, 900, 1,100 mm) are also available.

Figure 6.3 Typical dimensions for food service industry equipment

Body height in cm	Optimal and recommended work surface heights			Installation height for refrigerator/ freezers, in cm	Installation height for ovens/ microwave ovens, in cm	Shelf heights reachable from a standing position, measured from floor in cm		
	Countertop, in cm	Cooktop, in cm	Sink, in cm			Base cabinet drawer	Wall cabinet	Tall cabinet
135	70		80	65–130	60–135	34	140	150
140	80	70	85	65–140	65–135	35	145	155
145	80	70	90	60–150	70–140	36	150	160
150	85	80	90	60–155	75–145	37	155	165
155	90	85	95	55–160	80–150	39	160	170
160	90	85	95	55–165	85–155	40	165	175
165	95	90	100	55–170	90–155	41	170	180
170	100	95	100	55–175	95–165	42	175	185
175	100	95	105	55–180	95–165	43	180	190
180	105	100		55–185	100–170	44	185	195
185	105	100		55–190	105–175	46	190	200

Table 6.2 Work surfaces and gripping heights

Per AMK – Arbeitsgemeinschaft Die Moderne Küche
(The Modern Kitchen Working Group)

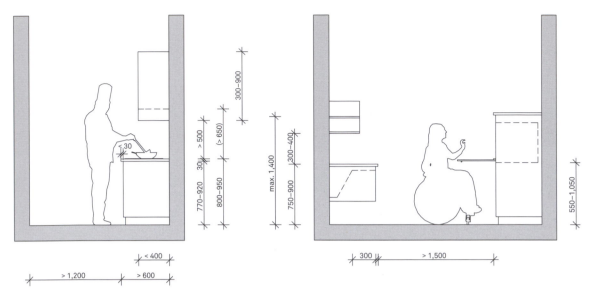

Figure 6.4 Wheelchair-accessible kitchen design

Comfort rule: The distance between work surface and elbow height should be 100–150 mm.
Dimension in parentheses: The clear distance above the cooktop must be a minimum of 650 mm. This is also recommended above the sink.

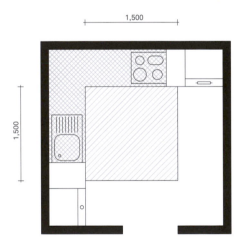

Figure 6.5 Wheelchair-accessible work areas and heights in kitchens

6.2 Private Kitchens

Kitchens in private residences have evolved from functional spaces designed for optimal efficiency to become a center of life at home. Communication between living, dining, and kitchen areas and the sense of amenity that goes along with it are important to many people, although individuals can have very different opinions of the advantages and disadvantages of open and closed kitchen concepts. Also when planning individual residential kitchens, minimum standards for clearances and areas should be observed. When planning for wheelchair accessibility, considerably larger kitchen areas are needed because adequate wheelchair clearance must be provided beneath counters and essential kitchen appliances such as the sink and stove, and because wall-hung cabinets are generally not accessible, thus requiring the provision of additional storage space at a height within reach.

Kitchen type	Recommended room size
Kitchenette within a room	approx. 5–6 m²
Kitchen for cooking only	approx. 8–10 m²
Eat-in kitchen	approx. 8–10 m², of which 5 m² is eating area for 4 people
Combined kitchen/living room	min. 15 m²

Table 6.3 Minimum areas for private kitchens

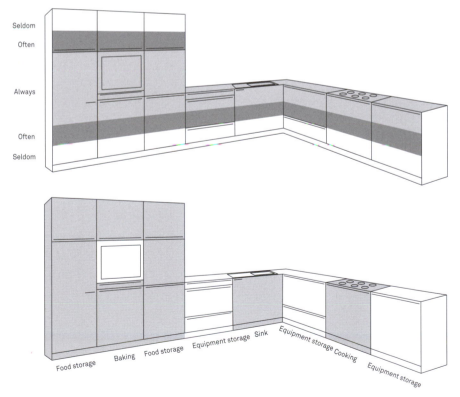

Figure 6.6 Zoning of kitchens

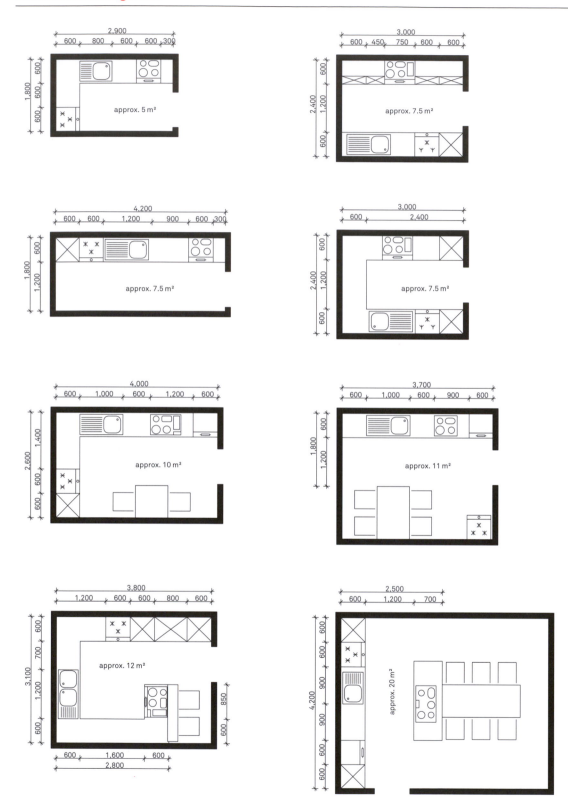

Figure 6.7 Examples for the layout of private kitchens

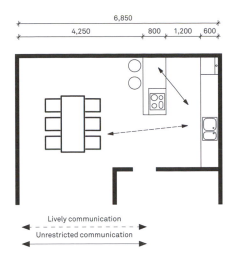

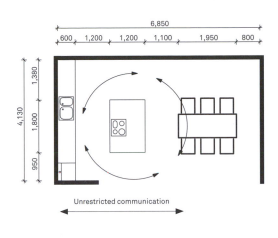

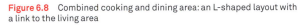

Figure 6.8 Combined cooking and dining area: an L-shaped layout with a link to the living area

Figure 6.9 Combination of a row of fitted kitchen furniture and a freestanding cooking island with dining area

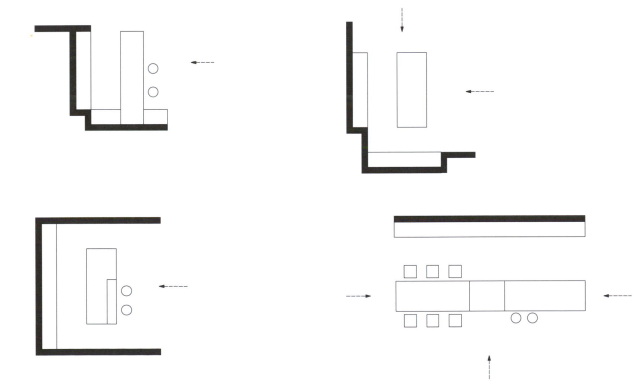

Figure 6.10 Examples of open-plan kitchens

6.3 Commercial Kitchens

The design of commercial kitchens is largely governed by building code, safety at work, and food hygiene regulations. Central kitchens are used to prepare food that is subsequently served via warm-up/satellite kitchens or distribution kitchens. Warm-up kitchens receive ready-prepared food in chilled or frozen form for reheating and serving. Distribution kitchens receive the food when it is already prepared and still warm so that it only needs to be kept warm until it is served. Other design considerations are the size of the kitchen, which depends on the number of portions to be prepared (small, medium, large kitchen).

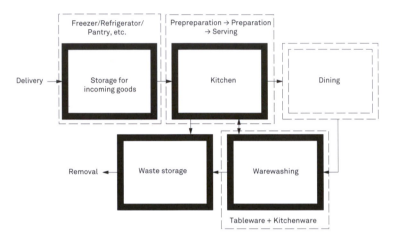

Figure 6.11   Functional areas and processes in commercial kitchens

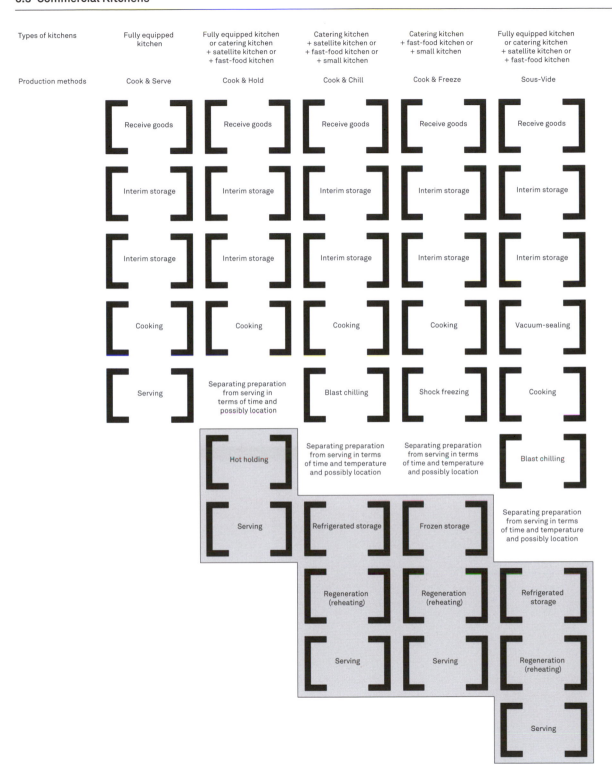

Figure 6.12 Processes of different production methods

Area	≤ 100 guests	≤ 250 guests	> 250 guests
Deliveries and waste removal	**0.2**	**0.2**	**0.2**
Receiving	0.07	0.06	0.05
Storage manager	0.03	0.02	0.04
Head chef's office	0.05	0.04	0.03
Waste storage	0.10	0.11	0.12
Goods storage	**0.35**	**0.45**	**0.38**
Prechilling room		0.03	0.03
Refrigerated storage – meat		0.05	0.04
Refrigerated storage – dairy		0.04	0.03
Refrigerated storage – vegetables		0.04	0.04
Walk-in freezer		0.04	0.04
Cold kitchen	0.02	0.02	
Food waste cold storage	0.02	0.02	
Dry storage	0.02	0.02	0.02
Vegetable storage	0.09	0.07	0.04
Beverage storage		0.03	0.02
Wine cellar		0.04	0.03
Tableware storage	0.04	0.03	0.03
Kitchen			
Meat preparation	0.1	0.08	0.05
Vegetable preparation	0.1	0.08	0.06
Hot kitchen	0.3	0.2	0.2
Cold kitchen (garde manger)	0.2	0.15	0.2
Assembly/portioning	0.08	0.08	0.07
Warewashing	0.1	0.12	0.1

Table 6.4 Guide values for kitchens and ancillary spaces, in m² per seat

Source: Alfons Goris, ed. *Schneider Bautabellen*, 18th ed. (2008)

6.4 Dining Areas

When planning dining areas, it is important to make sure that tables and chairs are arranged with sufficient space for movement so that the users do not interfere with one another while eating: attention must be given to ensure sufficient spacing between the individual chairs, sufficient dimensions for the areas surrounding the tables, and that people have the possibility to pass behind seated guests.

Especially for dining rooms with many tables, paths giving access to the tables should be laid out to avoid impediments by varying the table spacing. To enable wheelchair use, adequate clearance beneath the table and a maneuvering area of 1.50 m × 1.50 m between the table and other furniture or confining parts of the building must be provided.

Dimensions for dining areas	Minimum	Comfortable
Center-to-center spacing of seats	min. 0.60–0.65 m	approx. 0.80 m
Depth of table space per person	min. 0.40 m	approx. 0.50–0.60 m
Distance between chair and wall	min. 0.30 m	approx. 0.50 m
Distance between chair and wall, walking past is possible	min. 0.60 m	approx. 0.90 m
Distance between chair and other furniture	min. 0.70 m	approx. 1.0 m

Table 6.5 Clearances behind chairs

Number of people and arrangement	Width of floor space, in m	Depth of floor space, in m	Floor space, in m²
2 people, seated opposite	1.80	0.80	1.44
2 people, seated at corner	1.30	1.30	1.69
4 people, 1 person per side	1.80	1.80	3.24
4 people, 2 people per side	1.80	1.20	2.16
4 people, round table	2.10	2.10	4.41
5 people, 1 person at head of table	1.80	1.80	3.24
5 people, 2 chairs + corner bench	1.80	1.90	3.42
6 people, 3 people per side	1.80	1.80	3.24
6 people, 1 person at each end	1.80	2.30	4.14
8 people, 4 people per side	1.80	2.40	4.32
8 people, 1 person at each end	1.80	2.80	5.04

Table 6.6 Minimum floor space for dining areas

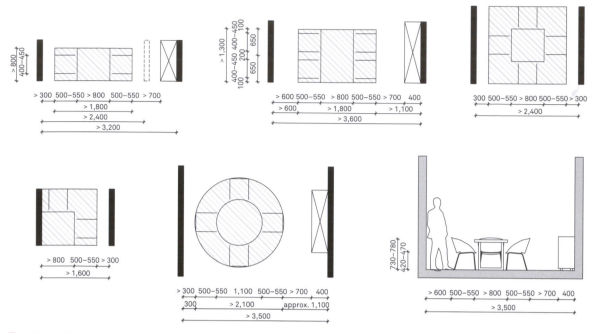

Figure 6.13 Minimum spacing in dining areas

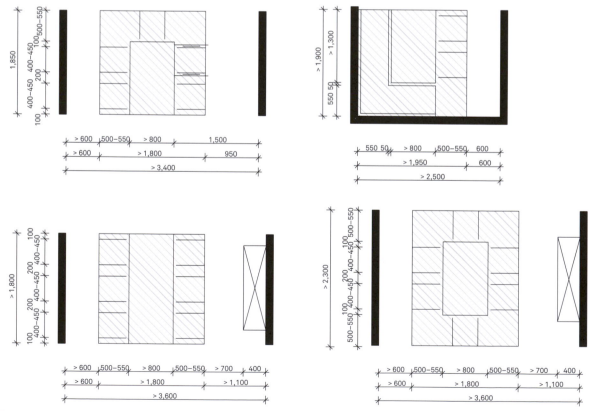

Figure 6.14 Typical table combinations

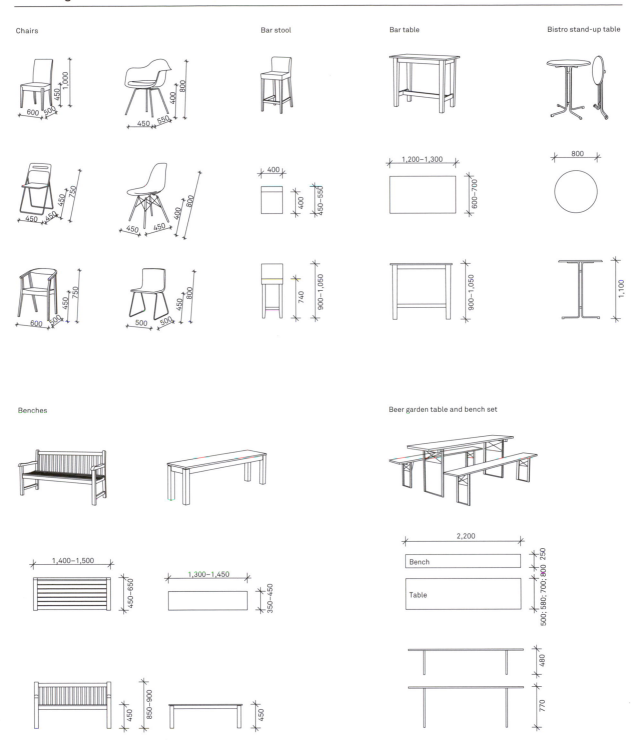

Chairs

Bar stool

Bar table

Bistro stand-up table

Benches

Beer garden table and bench set

Bench

Table

Figure 6.15 Seating elements and stand-up tables

7 Sanitary Facilities and Ancillary Rooms

When planning sanitary facilities, there are significant differences to be taken into account between private bathrooms and public or commercial/operational sanitary facilities. Although minimum dimensions for clearance distances and maneuvering zones apply, private bathrooms are nevertheless usually designed to also create agreeable surroundings.

As a rule, the planner should take into account the needs of wheelchair users by incorporating suitable accessibility of the plumbing fixtures into the sanitary planning. For publicly accessible facilities, requirements for safety and operation from a wheelchair must be observed. These include: Wheelchair clearance beneath lavatories; mirror at low height or tilted appropriately; shower areas without raised thresholds; seats and grab bars; space for wheelchair next to toilets and showers; toilets at wheelchair height and fitted with hinged grab bars; accessibility of all operating elements (shower controls, toilet paper holder, soap dispenser, etc.); alarm devices on all plumbing fixtures; slip resistance of the flooring; and doors that do not open inward.

Wheelchair-accessible water closets in public facilities must be approachable from both sides, whereas access from one side is generally sufficient for private bathrooms.

7.1 Plumbing Fixtures

For plumbing fixtures, typical widths, depths, mounting heights, and maneuvering areas must be taken into consideration. These are to be considered as minimums, however, and can be increased commensurate to the building typology and the amount of expected use of the plumbing fixture. Especially in public buildings such as trade fairs, theaters, sports venues, etc., where high numbers of users can be expected simultaneously, considerably larger maneuvering zones should be planned.

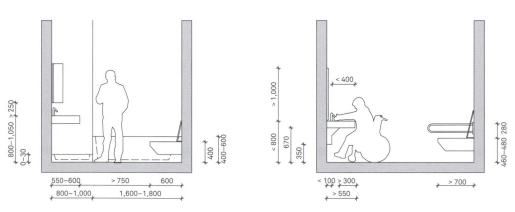

Figure 7.1   Heights of plumbing fixtures

Plumbing fixture	Floor space w × d (for standard sizes)	Maneuvering area in front of the fixture w × d (when opposite each other)	Side clearance	Height above finished floor
Single basin lavatory	600 × 550	900 × 550 (900 × 750)	200	800–950
Double basin lavatory	1,200 × 550	1,500 × 550 (1,500 × 750)	200	800–950
Lavatory	450 × 350	700 × 450 (700 × 750)	200 (250 with walls at both sides)	800–950
WC (flush tank in wall)	400 × 600	800 × 550 (800 × 750)	200 (250 with walls at both sides)	400
WC (flush tank in front of wall)	400 × 750	800 × 550 (800 × 750)	200 (250 with walls at both sides)	400
Urinal	400 × 400	600 × 600 (600 × 750)	200 (250 with walls at both sides)	650–700
Shower basin	800 × 800	800 × 750	200 (space between lavatory and shower basin can be reduced to 0)	0–30 (depending on model and type)
Bathtub	750 × 1,700	900 × 750	200 (space between lavatory and bathtub can be reduced to 0)	400–600 (ideal 590)

Table 7.1 Minimum dimensions of plumbing fixtures and maneuvering zones

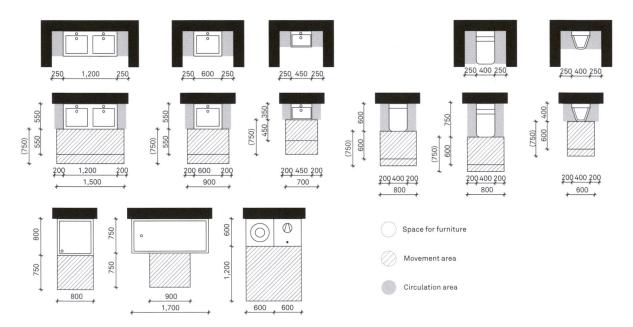

Figure 7.2 Plumbing fixtures and minimum dimensions of maneuvering zones

When laying out plumbing fixtures along a wall, larger clearances should be provided in order to ensure freedom of movement. Where plumbing fixtures are placed opposite each other, the extended maneuvering areas apply (values in parentheses).

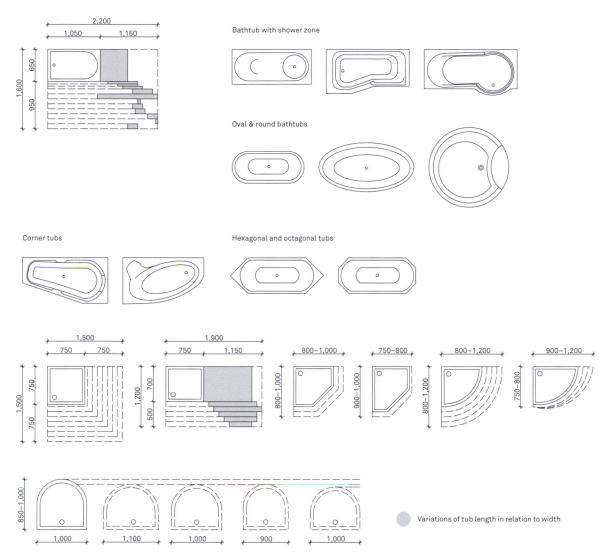

Figure 7.3 Common shapes and sizes of showers and bathtubs

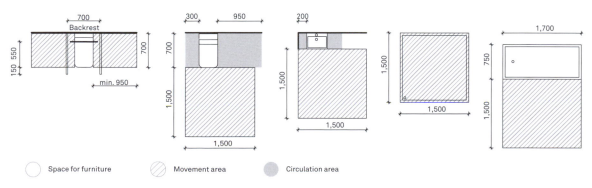

○ Space for furniture　▨ Movement area　● Circulation area

Figure 7.4 Wheelchair-accessible plumbing fixtures and minimum dimensions of maneuvering zones

Figure 7.5   Minimum dimensions for double wall construction

Figure 7.6   Typical arrangements of supply and drain lines for plumbing fixtures

7.2 Bathrooms and Private Sanitary Facilities

Private bathrooms and toilets are usually designed according to individual user requirements. Minimum requirements for clearances and maneuvering zones can play a decisive role in planning rental apartments. A spatial separation between the toilet and other plumbing fixtures is often made, or individual plumbing fixtures such as the bathtub are showcased as space-defining elements. In addition to accommodating the plumbing fixtures, sufficient space should also be planned for cabinets and shelf space. Furthermore, washing machines and dryers may need to be integrated if no other places are available for their installation.

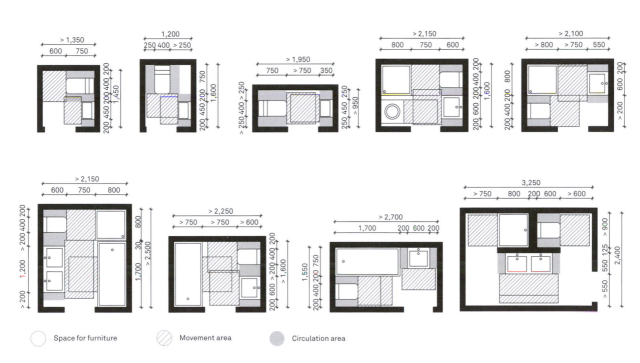

- ⬤ Space for furniture
- ◩ Movement area
- ⬤ Circulation area

Figure 7.7 Examples of minimum requirements for private toilets and bathrooms

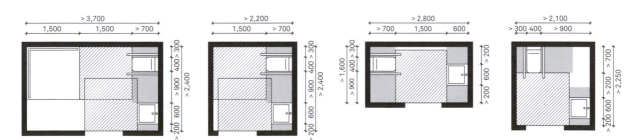

Figure 7.8 Layout of wheelchair-accessible toilets and shower rooms

7.3 Public and Commercial Sanitary Facilities

Public and commercial or industrial sanitary facilities must be laid out in sufficient numbers and within reasonable distances. With a view toward barrier-free accessibility, toilet cores should be designed to be unobstructed and bright and to have separate wheelchair-accessible toilets. These can be accommodated in a separate room or integrated into a larger facility with due regard to the specific requirements. The quantity of necessary plumbing fixtures is specified by the requirements of public law (for example, occupational safety and health standards). Women's and men's toilets, a (unisex) wheelchair-accessible toilet and/ or baby changing rooms as well as janitor's closets, if required, are combined in sanitary cores. The planner must take into account that sometimes there may be several people occupying the same area, such as the space in front of the sinks. All the same, privacy must be maintained, by not permitting direct views from the corridor into the toilet areas when the doors open, for instance, and by providing a separate anteroom for the sinks. The provision of screen walls and toilet partitions as well as privacy screens at the urinals ensures sufficient privacy within the toilet room.

In public toilet cores, baby changing areas for infants should always be provided in separate rooms. Washrooms and shower areas (for example, in production plants, sports facilities, or technical buildings) can be designed with individual stalls or as a group area, depending on the requirements, and combined with a communal changing room with or without partitions. In any case, sufficient shelf space and clothing hooks must be provided and transition zones must be planned between wet and dry areas.

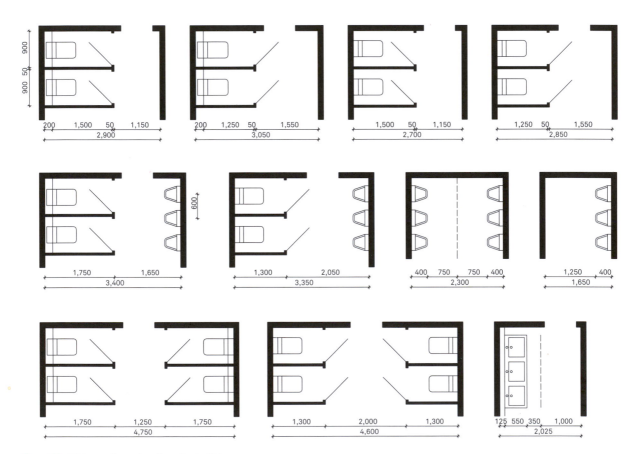

Figure 7.9 Minimum dimensions for toilet facilities

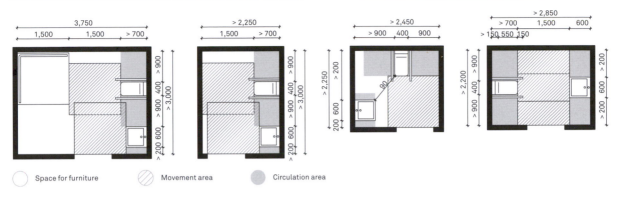

○ Space for furniture   ◨ Movement area   ◉ Circulation area

Figure 7.10 Wheelchair-accessible toilets and shower rooms (publicly accessible)

Figure 7.11 Examples of the layout of toilet cores

87

Figure 7.12   Requirements and layout of washing and shower areas

Per ASR A4.1
a) open rows of showers and shower stalls
b) shower stalls with visual screening/splash protection
c) shower stalls with double T-shaped visual screening/splash protection
d) row of individual shower stalls with private drying areas
e) row of shower stalls with shared drying area
f) wash positions

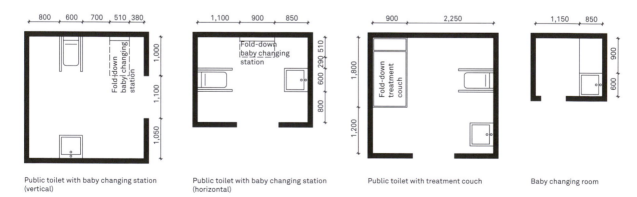

Public toilet with baby changing station
(vertical)

Public toilet with baby changing station
(horizontal)

Public toilet with treatment couch

Baby changing room

Figure 7.13   Baby changing areas in toilet facilities

Workplaces	Reference unit (RU)	Number of plumbing fixtures				
Requirements as per VDI 6000 Part 2						
	Number of all employees	WCs (women)	Lavatories	WCs (men)	Urinals	Lavatories
Total number of employees is known	6–10	1	1	1	1	1
	11–20	1	1	1	1	1
	21–50	2	2	1	2	2
	51–75	2	2	2	3	2
	76–100	4	2	2	4	2
	101–150	5	3	2	5	3
	151–200	7	3	3	7	4
	201–250	8	4	4	8	5
	Number of employees (female and male)	WCs (women)	Lavatories	WCs (men)	Urinals	Lavatories
Respective numbers of male and female employees is known	6–10	1	1	1	1	1
	11–20	2	1	1	2	1
	21–50	2	1	2	2	2
	51–75	4	2	2	4	2
	76–100	5	3	2	5	3
	101–150	7	3	3	7	4
	151–200	8	4	4	8	5
	201–250	10	5	5	10	5

Table 7.2   Various minimum requirements for plumbing fixtures in workplaces

Requirements as per ASR A4.1				
Female or male employees	Minimum number for low concurrence (values apply for men and women)		Minimum number for high concurrence (values apply for men and women)	
	WCs/urinals	Lavatories	WCs/urinals	Lavatories
max. 5	1 (for male employees: 1 addtl. urinal)	1	2	1
6–10	1 (for male employees: 1 addtl. urinal)	1	3	1
11–25	2	1	4	2
26–50	3	1	6	2
51–75	5	2	7	3
76–100	6	2	9	3
101–130	7	3	11	4
131–160	8	3	13	4
161–190	9	3	15	5
191–220	10	4	17	6
221–250	11	4	19	7
	+ 1 for each addtl. 30 employees	+ 1 for each addtl. 90 employees	+ 2 for each addtl. 30 employees	+ 2 for each addtl. 90 employees

Table 7.2 (continuation) Various minimum requirements for plumbing fixtures in workplaces

Visitors	WCs (women)	Lavatories	WCs (men)	Urinals	Lavatories
Low concurrence					
25	1	1	1	1	1
50/100	2	2	1	2	1/2
300/500	4	2/3	2	4	2/3
700	5	4	3	5	4
1,000	6	4	4	6	5
1,500	8	6	5	8	6
2,000	9	7	6	9	8

- Overall, 1 toilet room each for women and men
- Max. 1,000 visitors: 1 barrier-free stall each for women and men
- Over 1,000 visitors: 2 barrier-free stalls each for women and men

Table 7.3 Minimum number of plumbing fixtures in places of assembly

As per VDI 6000
Statutory requirements such as regulations governing places of assembly can impose considerably higher requirements. Here, 0.8–1.2 WCs per 100 visitors are required, and the quantities may be reduced depending on the total number. The legal requirements applicable for the project site must therefore be verified in each instance!

Visitors	WCs (women)	Lavatories	WCs (men)	Urinals	Lavatories
Average concurrence					
25	1	1	1	1	1
50	2	2	1	2	1
100	3	3	1	3	2
300	5	3	2	5	3
500	6	4	3	6	4
700	7	5	4	7	5
1,000	9	6	5	9	7
1,500	11	8	7	11	9
2,000	13	10	9	13	11

- Max. 1,000 visitors: 1 toilet room each for women and men and 1 barrier-free stall each for women and men
- Over 1,000 visitors: 2 toilet rooms each for women and men and 2 barrier-free stalls each for women and men

Visitors	WCs (women)	Lavatories	WCs (men)	Urinals	Lavatories
High concurrence					
25	2	2	2	2	2
50	3	3	2	3	2
100	5	5	2	5	3
300	8	5	3	8	5
500	9	6	5	9	6
700	11	8	6	11	8
1,000	14	9	8	14	11
1,500	17	12	11	17	14
2,000	20	15	14	20	17

- Max. 500 visitors: 1 toilet room each for women and men
- Over 500 visitors: 2 toilet rooms each for women and men
- Max. 1,000 visitors: 1 barrier-free stall each for women and men
- Over 1,000 visitors: 2 barrier-free stalls each for women and men

Table 7.3 (continuation)   Minimum number of plumbing fixtures in places of assembly

As per VDI 6000
Statutory requirements such as regulations governing places of assembly can impose considerably higher requirements. Here, 0.8–1.2 WCs per 100 visitors are required, and the quantities may be reduced depending on the total number. The legal requirements applicable for the project site must therefore be verified in each instance!

7.4 Locker and Changing Rooms

Depending on the building typology, locker and changing areas fulfill various purposes and must consequently be planned accordingly. They can, for instance, be combined with a toilet and shower area for users of sports facilities or serve as a warm-up area for actors in a theater. Changing areas are often needed in work environments for hygienic reasons or when it is mandatory to wear uniforms. The spectrum ranges from simple lockers in staff rooms to hermetic separation between clean and dirty areas. Such changing areas serve as vestibules between work areas and the outside.

Layout of swimming pool locker room

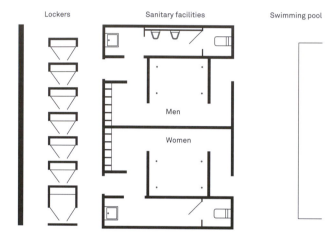

Layout of gymnasium locker room

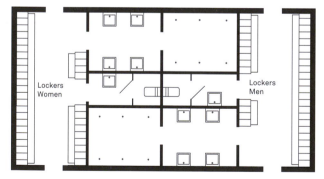

Figure 7.14   Changing areas serving as access control

7.4 Locker and Changing Rooms

Layout of a clean/dirty locker room

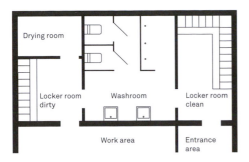

Figure 7.15 Staff changing areas

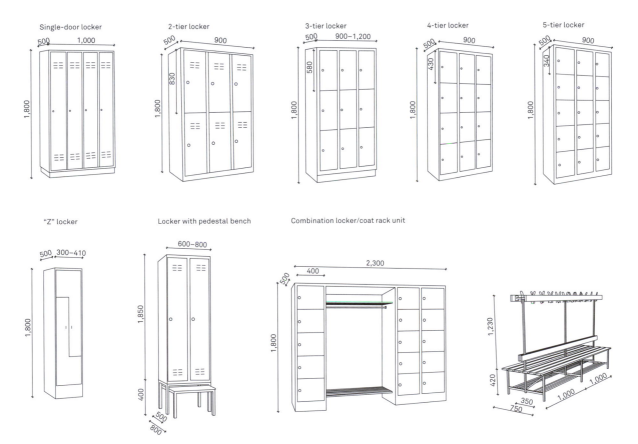

Figure 7.16 Various locker systems

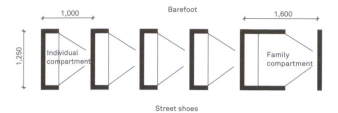

Figure 7.17 Principle of changing compartments (e.g., in swimming pools)

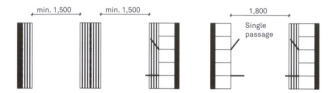

Figure 7.18 Maneuvering zones in changing rooms

For changing areas, a bench surface of min. 400 mm wide and 300 mm deep shall be provided. For wheelchair users, additional transfer areas shall be provided. The circulation space between benches must be at least 1,500 mm wide. If the path serves as the only passage, 1,800 mm shall be provided.

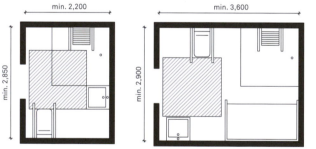

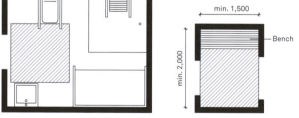

Figure 7.19 Changing areas for wheelchair users

For people with disabilities, accessible individual stalls measuring a minimum of 1,500 × 2,000 mm shall be provided commensurate with the need. Including WC, shower, folding seat, and sink, a minimum of 2,200 × 2,850 mm (without examination table) or 2,900 × 3,600 mm (with examination table) shall be provided.

Changing room facilities with lockers

Lockers without bench

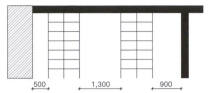

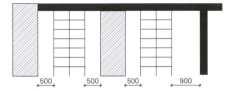

Lockers with bench

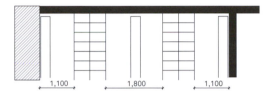

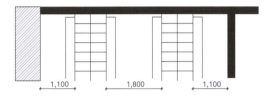

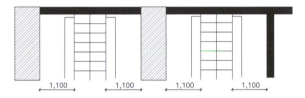

Lockers with kick plate

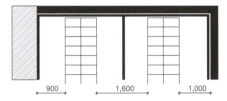

Lockers with movable stools

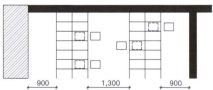

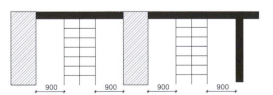

Figure 7.20 Layouts of changing and locker rooms
Per Ordinance on Workplaces, §34

Changing room facilities with base frames

Simple hook racks

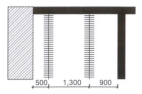

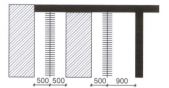

Coat hanger racks

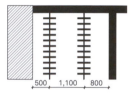

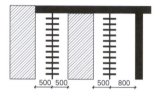

Coat hanger racks with kick plate

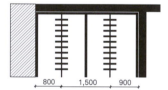

Changing room facilities with attended cloakroom (theater cloakroom)

Attended cloakroom, single-sided, with hook rack

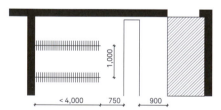

Attended cloakroom, double-sided, with coat hanger rack

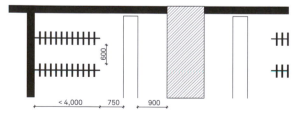

Benches in attended cloakrooms

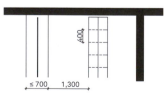

Figure 7.21 Layouts of cloakroom areas

Per Ordinance on Workplaces, §34

7.5 Medical and First Aid Rooms

A first aid room is a room where, in the event of an accident, emergency medical care can be provided until the ambulance service arrives, if required. It should be centrally located on the ground floor in order to ensure quick access, even with stretchers. First aid rooms must have an area of at least 20 m² and a clear height of 2.50 m. They contain the following minimum furnishings and equipment: examination table, dressing trolley, sink with hot and cold water, mirror, soap and disinfectant dispensers, emergency light, telephone, desk, and stretcher as well as sundry first aid materials. There must be a shower and a toilet with direct access from the first aid room, or at least in close proximity to it.

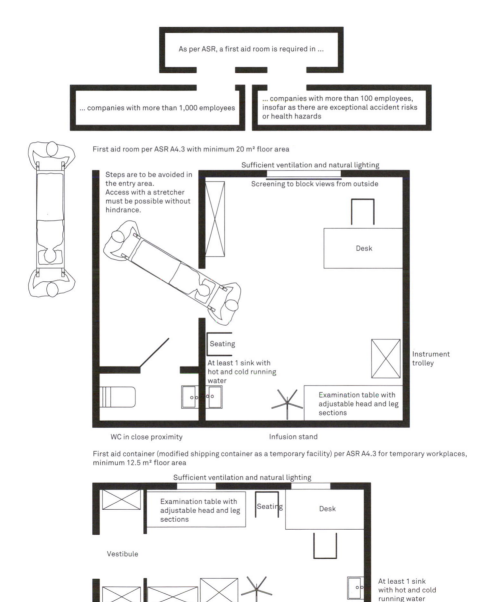

As per ASR, a first aid room is required in ...

... companies with more than 1,000 employees

... companies with more than 100 employees, insofar as there are exceptional accident risks or health hazards

First aid room per ASR A4.3 with minimum 20 m² floor area

Sufficient ventilation and natural lighting

Steps are to be avoided in the entry area.
Access with a stretcher must be possible without hindrance.

Screening to block views from outside

Desk

Seating

At least 1 sink with hot and cold running water

Instrument trolley

Examination table with adjustable head and leg sections

WC in close proximity

Infusion stand

First aid container (modified shipping container as a temporary facility) per ASR A4.3 for temporary workplaces, minimum 12.5 m² floor area

Sufficient ventilation and natural lighting

Examination table with adjustable head and leg sections

Seating

Desk

Vestibule

At least 1 sink with hot and cold running water

Instrument trolley

Infusion stand

Figure 7.22 First aid room
Per ASR A4.3

8 Work Environments

Workrooms and production spaces are decisively governed by regulations for occupational safety, which are increasingly being standardized internationally and cover all facets of workplace activities. With respect to architectural matters, occupational health and safety regulations impose many requirements on spaces, materials, safety devices, and the physical conditions of the workplace.

8.1 Workplaces

In addition to providing protection against occupational accidents and safeguarding health, the work environment plays an important role in ensuring the well-being and productivity of workers. The stresses encountered while working are very diverse: the work might be accomplished while sitting, standing, or in motion, and it might require an unvaried posture or be physically strenuous. It can be char-

acterized by manual work with one's hands, subservient to production rhythms, or performed as a service that predominantly requires work on a computer. For each specific mode of working, the most optimal environment possible must be ensured in terms of anthropometric requirements, room temperature, natural lighting, etc. In this regard, the requirements for computer workstations are very specific.

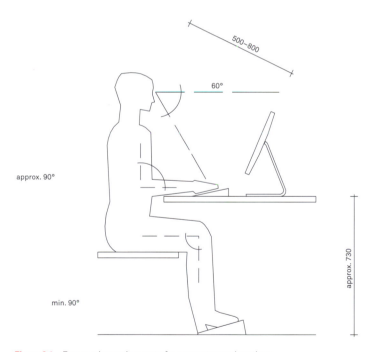

Figure 8.1   Ergonomic requirements for computer workstations

Minimum ceiling height for workrooms	
Floor area	Clear ceiling height
< 50 m²	2.50 m
50–100 m²	2.75 m
> 100 m²	3.00 m
> 2,000 m²	3.25 m

Table 8.1 Minimum ceiling heights for workrooms
Per ASR A1.2

Working heights and table heights for various types of standing work		
Type of work	Working height	Table height
Fine work	1,200–1,500 mm	1,200–1,500 mm
Light work	950–1,200 mm	900–1,150 mm
Heavy work	900–1,150 mm	750–1,050 mm

Table 8.2 Working heights and table heights
Per DGUV

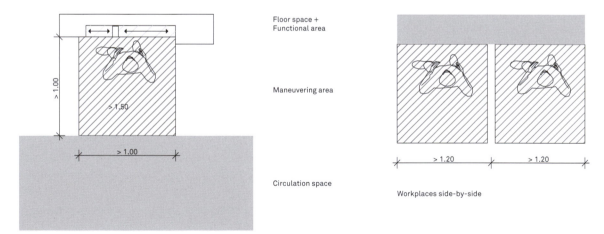

Floor space +
Functional area

Maneuvering area

Circulation space

Workplaces side-by-side

Figure 8.2 Requisite maneuvering areas
Based on the Technical Rules for Workplaces (ASR A1.8/Circulation areas) and the Model Industrial Buildings Directive (M-IndBauRL)

8.2 Office Spaces

The following basic forms of office layouts can be distinguished: cellular offices, group offices, open-plan offices, and combi-offices. In addition, it is possible to combine the above types of layouts in order to create more varied office landscapes. The design of workrooms for highly qualified employees in particular tries to ensure that these staff members are comfortable at their workplaces and can choose between different options to suit their preferences or type of activity.

Properties	Cellular offices	Group offices	Combi-offices	Open-plan offices
Number of workplaces	1–4 persons	Usually 8–12, small groups 5–8, max. 20–25 persons	Flexible design, see cellular/group offices	From 25 persons, often more than 100 persons
Room depths	Approx. 5.00 to 6.00 m	Approx. 5.00 to 10.00 m	See cellular/group offices + approx. 5.00 to 7.00 m for the combi-zone	Varies, usually approx. 15.00 to 30.00 m
Room widths	Approx. 2.60 to 5.00 m	Approx. 7.00 to 30.00 m	Flexible design, see cellular/group offices	Varies, usually up to approx. 40.00 m
Used for	Administration and office workers, service areas with external customers, leading management staff, managing director	Team-oriented and networked working in small groups	Suitable for a range of different staff structures owing to the varied spaces	Administration and office workers, call centers, IT services
Working atmosphere	Quiet, individual, uncommunicative	Team-oriented, communicative, can be noisy	Team work and meetings in the combi-zone; concentrated work in cellular offices is also possible due to the combination cellular, group, and open-plan offices	Good communication, but usually acoustic and visual disruptions, impersonal work environment
Personal choice of workplace design	Individual design is possible	Restricted to the respective desk space	See cellular/group offices	Restricted to the respective desk space
Services installation	Possible via partitions or wall-mounted ducts	Via floor ducts, raised floors and floor boxes, or suspended ceilings	Via floor ducts, raised floors and floor boxes, or suspended ceilings	Congested installation in suspended ceilings and raised floors
Lighting	Natural/artificial, can be individually controlled	Natural/artificial, can be controlled by the group	Natural near the facade/artificial at greater distance from the facade	Only artificial possible
Ventilation	Natural/artificial, can be individually controlled	Natural (small groups), otherwise artificial, can be controlled by the group	Natural possible near the facade/artificial at greater distance from the facade	Only artificial possible

Table 8.3 Comparison of the properties of different office types

Workroom for one person	≥ 8 m²
Workroom for two persons	≥ 13 m²
Workroom for three persons	≥ 18 m²
Each additional workplace	+ ≥ 5 m²

Table 8.4 Approximate minimum space requirements

Unobstructed movement area	1.50 m²
Minimum depth of personally assigned workplace	1.00 m
Minimum depth of other workplaces	0.80 m
Minimum depth of visitor/meeting places	0.80 m

Table 8.5 User areas around desks
Per ArbStättV

Office layout type		Persons	Room depth	Room height
Cellular office		1 to 4	5 to 7 m	≥ 2.50 m
Group office		5 to 25	5 to 10 m	≥ 2.50 to ≥ 3.00 m
	Small groups	5 to 8	5 to 7.5 m	≥ 2.50 to ≥ 2.75 m
	Large groups	8 to 25	7.5 to 10 m	≥ 2.75 to ≥ 3.00 m
Combi-office (cellular and group offices)		1 to 25	5 to 10 m	≥ 2.75 to ≥ 3.00 m
Open-plan office		25 to > 100	15 to 30 m	≥ 3.00 to ≥ 3.25 m

Table 8.6 Depth and height of rooms of different basic office layout types

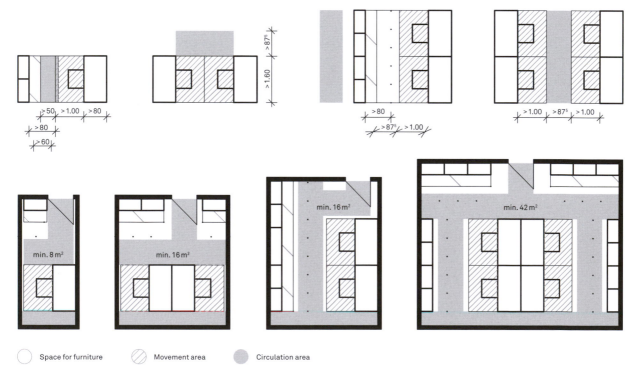

○ Space for furniture   ◇ Movement area   ● Circulation area

Figure 8.3 Minimum space requirement for workplaces

8.3 Lunchrooms

Lunchrooms and break areas give employees a place to stay during work breaks. A minimum of 1 m² per employee is to be provided in addition to the circulation spaces and fixed furniture, with a minimum room size of 6 m². Each lunchroom must have a visual connection to the outside and receive sufficient natural light. If there is no staff canteen or similar facility, employees should be given the opportunity to prepare their own meals or to heat them up in the lunchroom.

Visual connection to outside and
sufficient daylight

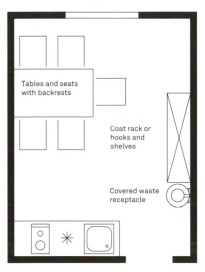

Tables and seats
with backrests

Coat rack or
hooks and
shelves

Covered waste
receptacle

– Access to drinking water
– Ability to refrigerate and warm up
   food if there is no canteen

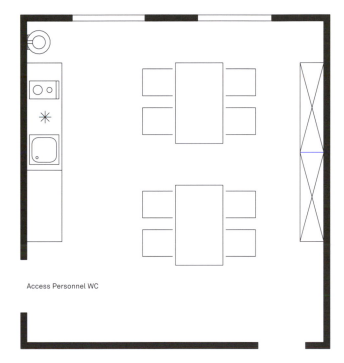

Access Personnel WC

Figure 8.4 Features of lunchrooms

Per ASR A4.2
Floor area: min. 6 m²
1 m²/user (incl. table and chair)
+ Entry/exit
+ Circulation space
+ Other facilities

9 Communication and Education Spaces

Communication spaces encompass a multitude of diverse activities and typological features in the educational, professional, and leisure sectors. For communication areas it is essential to creatively bring about the implemented or desired cultures of encounter and interaction in order to also convey these intuitively to nonlocal users. For example, the seating arrangement in a seminar or conference room plays an essential role in determining how easily a free and uninhibited discussion can develop. Similarly, the design of waiting areas has considerable influence on the length of waiting time that is perceived as acceptable.

9.1 Lecture, Seminar, and Conference Rooms

The area requirements for lecture rooms, classrooms, seminar rooms, and conference rooms are directly dependent on the method of communication. Depending on the typology or business segment, highly varied concepts of teaching and communication methods are used, such as presentation style (that is, lecture-style instruction), group projects, panel discussions, guided discussions, free exchange of opinions, etc. For planning and design purposes, it is important to know if the communication processes will be guided or free and democratic, and which furniture layouts are desired for the purpose. Meeting rooms for up to three persons do not require special technical equipment. In meeting rooms for up to twelve persons it may be necessary to provide not only tables and chairs but also a screen or monitor, and computer connections for networking. All rooms with screens and monitors should have a black-out facility. Rooms that can be divided need separate doors to the corridor. Furthermore, both parts of the room should be adequately provided with furniture and media equipment.

Number of persons	Area in m²
50	60–70
100	90–110
120	120–130
150	150–200
200	≥200
300	≥350
400	≥400
500	≥500
700	≥700
1,200	≥800

Table 9.1 Rough size of a lecture hall as a function of the number of people accommodated

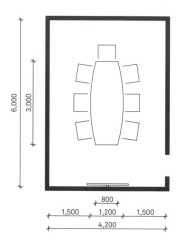

Figure 9.1 Example of furniture layout in a small meeting room

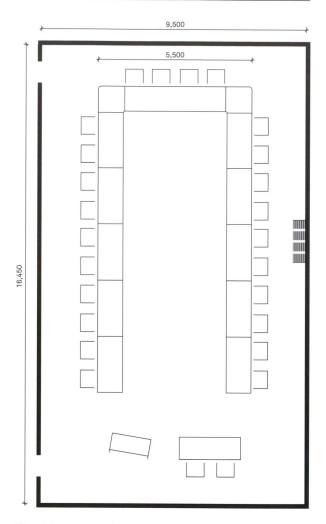

Figure 9.2 Example of (U-shaped) furniture layout in a large conference room

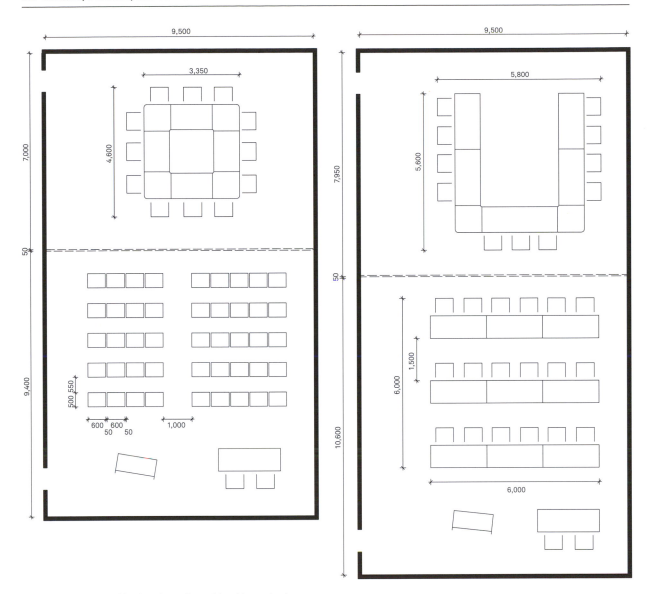

Figure 9.3 Examples of furniture layout in partitionable meeting/
conference rooms

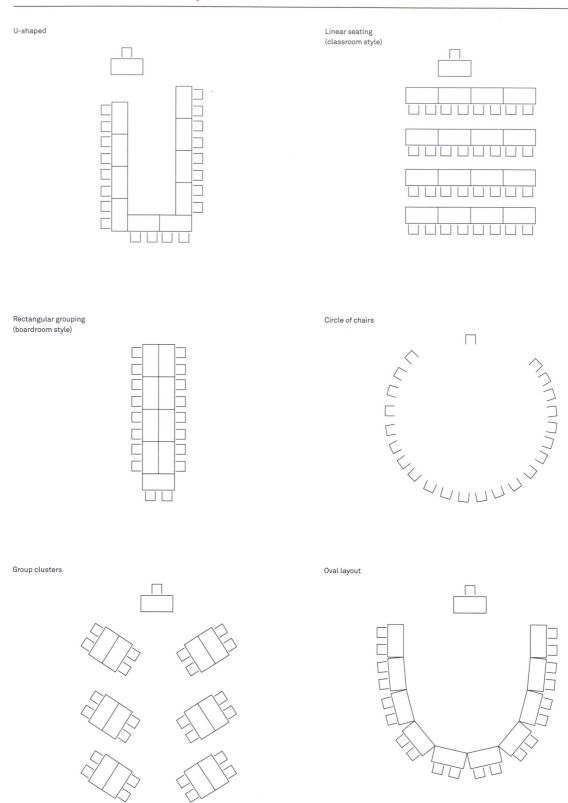

U-shaped

Linear seating
(classroom style)

Rectangular grouping
(boardroom style)

Circle of chairs

Group clusters

Oval layout

Figure 9.4 Seminar and conference seating

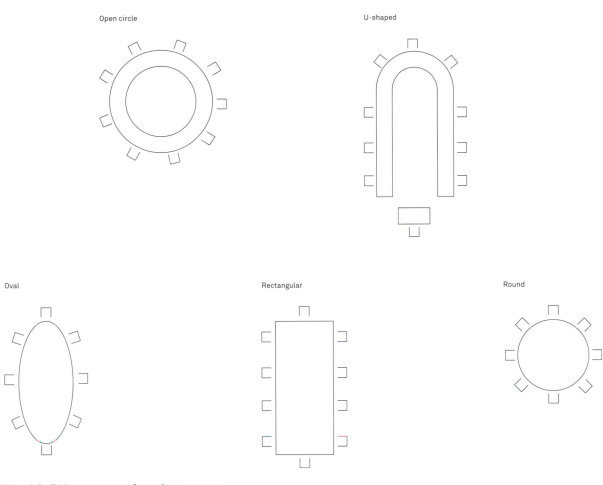

Figure 9.5 Table arrangements for conference rooms

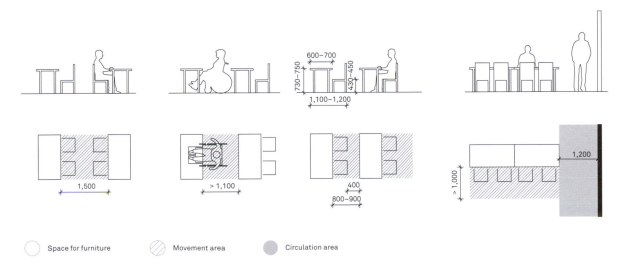

Figure 9.6 Seating furniture in lecture halls and lecture rooms

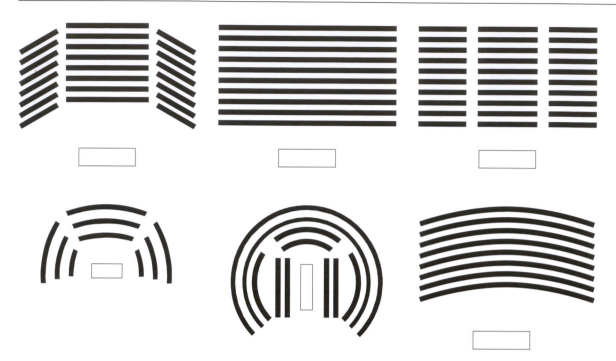

Figure 9.7 Layout of seating rows in lecture halls and lecture rooms

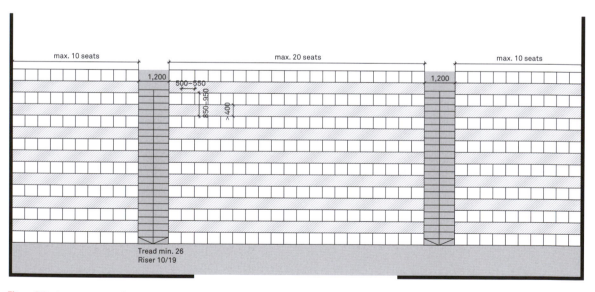

Figure 9.8 Access to rows of seats

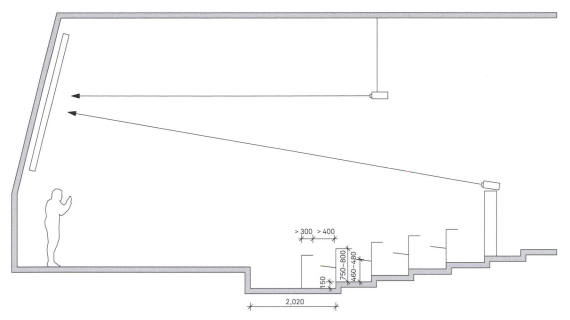

Figure 9.9 Tiered seating in lecture halls and lecture rooms

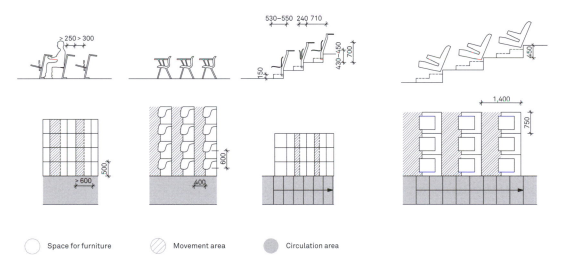

⊙ Space for furniture   ⊘ Movement area   ● Circulation area

Figure 9.10 Seating furniture in lecture halls and lecture rooms

Laboratory bench

Lectern

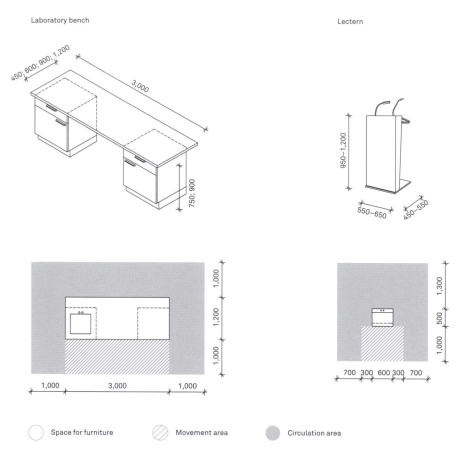

○ Space for furniture   ▨ Movement area   ● Circulation area

Figure 9.11   Lecterns and laboratory benches in lecture halls and lecture rooms

Examples of seating arrangements for 24 students in lessons

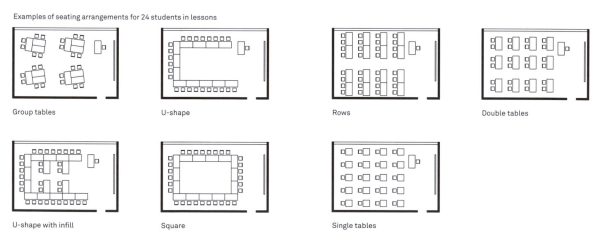

Group tables

U-shape

Rows

Double tables

U-shape with infill

Square

Single tables

Figure 9.12   Furnishing examples for classrooms

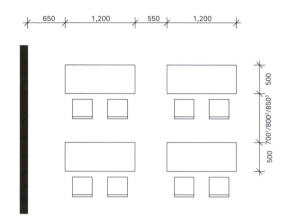

Figure 9.13 Minimum dimensions for the arrangement of tables in teaching rooms

1 For 6-to-10-year-olds with max. 2 seats next to each other
2 For 10-to-19-year-olds with max. 2 seats next to each other or
   6-to-10-year-olds with more than 2 seats next to each other
3 For 10-to-19-year-old students with more than 2 places next
   to each other

Grade	1	1–4	2–7	5–13	7–13	9–13
Seating height[1]	310	350	380	430	460	510
Effective seating depth[2]	270	300	340	360	380	400
Seating width[3]	280	320	340	360	380	400
Height of tabletop[2]	530	590	640	710	760	820
Maximum depth of tabletop	500[5]	500[5]	500	500	500	500
Maximum length of tabletop[4]	600[6]	600[6]	600[6]	600	600	600

Table 9.2 Size categories of tables and chairs in educational institutions (dimensions in mm)

1 ± 10 mm for chairs with a seat inclination between – 5° and + 5°
2 ± 10 mm for tables for use with chairs with a seat inclination between – 5° and + 5°
3 At least
4 Per user
5 Can be reduced to 400 mm
   (only if necessary due to confined space).
6 Can be reduced to 550 mm
   (only if necessary due to confined space).

9.2 Waiting and Seating Areas

Gathering places and seating areas should be commensurate in terms of density and size with the anticipated number of people and the expectations with regard to the typology. Thus seating areas in private apartments differ greatly from waiting areas at public agencies, infrastructure buildings such as train stations or airports, and medical facilities, or break areas in cultural and recreational facilities. At peak times (before or after theater performances, for example) or for large numbers of people over brief periods of time (at airport gates, for example), areas for sitting and waiting in line should be sufficiently differentiated. For cultural and recreational buildings, combining gathering places and seating areas with food service offerings is also desirable.

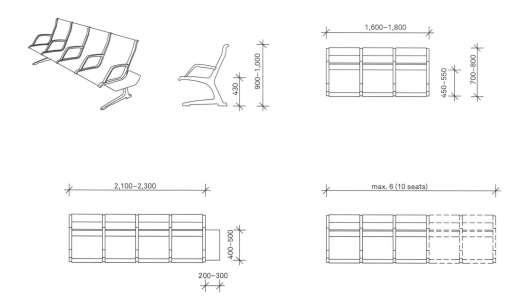

Figure 9.14   Space requirements for seating rows

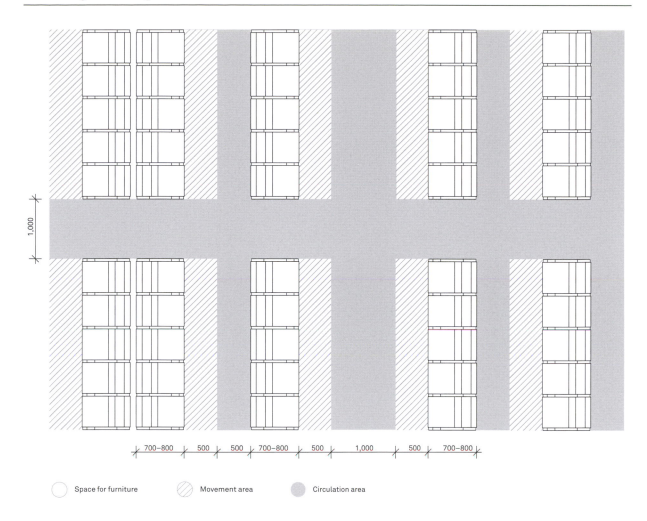

Space for furniture   Movement area   Circulation area

Figure 9.15 Space requirements for waiting areas

10 Sports and Recreation Facilities

The design and outward configuration of buildings for sports and recreation strongly reflect the activities they accommodate. They can be designed specifically for a particular sport or made to be multifunctional and flexible. The spectrum ranges from clubhouses, gymnasiums, and indoor swimming pools to major projects like multifunctional stadiums.

10.1 Sports Areas

The areas needed for the specific sports that will be played constitute the starting point for the design of sports buildings. Generally, the dimensions and ceiling heights needed for the actual sports areas (for instance, a playing field, court, or lane) are specified by the pertinent sport associations or the provisions of applicable standards, which are supplemented by perimeter areas to allow for safety clearances and free movement. The arrangement of the neces-sary auxiliary areas, such as changing rooms, equipment storage, and areas for building services, must be such that the shortest possible circulation paths result along with clearly definable zoning. If spectator areas are needed, not only are tiered seating areas along the playing field required, but also additional facilities such as sanitary facilities solely for public use, food service, separate entrances with access control, ticket booths, etc.

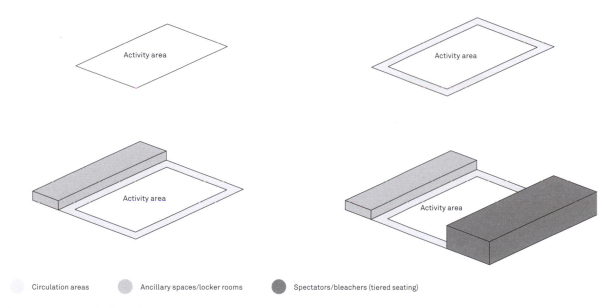

○ Circulation areas   ○ Ancillary spaces/locker rooms   ● Spectators/bleachers (tiered seating)

Figure 10.1   Systematization of the space requirements

Sport	Area of playing field, court, or lane/track			Delineated space including clearances			Clear height	Remarks
	Length	Width	Area	Length	Width	Area		
Acrobatic gymnastics	12.00 m	12.00 m	144 m²	14.00 m	14.00 m	196 m²	5.50 m	
American football	109.72 m	48.76 m	5,350 m²	113.75 m	50.80 m	5,779 m²		
Apparatus gymnastics	29.00 m	16.00 m	464 m²	36.00 m	16.00 m	576 m²	7.00 m	For national and international events: 1 m clearance required on the long sides and 3 m at the ends
Archery	30.00–90.00 m	4.00–5.00 m	120–450 m²	280.00–340.00 m	4.00–5.00 m	1,120–1,700 m²		
Artistic (trick) cycling	14.00 m	11.00 m	154 m²	16.00–18.00 m	11.00–13.00 m	176–234 m²	4.00 m	
Badminton	13.40 m	6.10 m	82 m²	15.50 m	6.70 m	122 m²	9.00 (7.00) m	7 m is sufficient for national events
Baseball	27.43 m	27.43 m	753 m²	121.92 m	121.92 m	14,864 m²		Diagonal playing direction
Basketball	28.00 m	15.00 m	420 m²	32.00 m	19.00 m	608 m²	7.00 m	
Beach ball	20.00–30.00 m	10.00–20.00 m	200–600 m²	30.00 m	20.00 m	600 m²		
Beachvolleyball	16.00 m	8.00 m	128 m²	22.00 m	14.00 m	308 m²		
Boules	27.50 m	2.50–4.00 m	69–110 m²	27.50 m	2.50–4.00 m	69–110 m²		
Bowling	19.20 m	1.06 m	20 m²	23.73 m	1.04 m	25 m²		
Boxing	4.90–6.10 m	4.90–6.10 m	24–38 m²	5.90–7.10 m	5.90–7.10 m	35–51 m²	4.00 m	
Casting	100.00 m	50.00 m	5,000 m²	100.00 m	50.00 m	5,000 m²		
Cricket	20.12 m	2.05 m	62 m²	150.00 m	90.00 m	13,500 m²		Field has elliptical shape
Curling	45.72 m	5.02 m	230 m²	46.00 m	6.25 m	269 m²	4.00–7.00 m	Min. 3 curling sheets per facility
Cycle ball/ cycle polo	14.00 m	11.00 m	154 m²	16.00–18.00 m	11.00–13.00 m	176–234 m²	4.00 m	
Darts	2.37 m	1.00 m	2.37 m²					Side clearance from sheet to wall: min. 0.90 m; between two sheets: min. 1.80 m
Dressage	20.00 m	40.00–60.00 m	800–1,200 m²	20.00 m	40.00–60.00 m	800–1,200 m²		Standardized dressage arena
Equestrianism (horseback riding)	16.00–25.00 m	20.00–65.00 m	320–1,625 m²	18.00–27.00 m	22.00–67.00 m	396–1,809 m²	4.40 m	
Fencing	14.00 m	1.50–2.00 m	21–48 m²	19.00–30.00 m	7.80–8.00 m	148–240 m²	4.00 m	

Table 10.1 Playing field sizes of various sports

Sport	Area of playing field, court, or lane/track			Delineated space including clearances			Clear height	Remarks
	Length	Width	Area	Length	Width	Area		
Field hockey	91.40 m	55.00 m	5,027 m²	101.40 m	63.00 m	6,389 m²	5.50 m	
Fistball	50.00 m	20.00 m	1,000 m²	66.00 m	32.00 m	2,112 m²		
Football tennis	12.80–18.00 m	8.20 m	105–148 m²	19.80–25.00 m	14.20 m	282–355 m²		
Futsal (five-a-side indoor soccer)	38.00–42.00 m	20.00–25.00 m	760–1,050 m²	39.00–46.00 m	21.00–26.00 m	819–1,196 m²		
Handball	40.00 m	20.00 m	800 m²	44.00 m	22.00 m	968 m²	7.00 m	
Ice hockey	60.00 m	26.00–30.00 m	1,560–1,800 m²	59.00–64.00 m	30.50–34.50 m	1,800–2,208 m²		3 m safety clearance at access area
Indoor hockey	36.00–44.00 m	18.00–22.00 m	648–968 m²	40.00–48.00 m	19.00–23.00 m	760–1,104 m²	5.50 m	
Judo	8.00–10.00 m	8.00–10.00 m	64–100 m²	14.00–16.00 m	14.00–16.00 m	196–256 m²	4.00 m	
Lacrosse	102.00 m	55.00 m	5,610 m²	115.00 m	60.00 m	6,900 m²		
Netball	30.00 m	15.00 m	450 m²	32.00 m	17.00 m	544 m²	5.50 m	
Nine-pin bowling	19.50 m	1.50 m	30 m²	25.00 m	1.50 m	38 m²		
Polo	274.00 m	146.00 m	40,004 m²	274.00 m	146.00 m	40,004 m²		
Rhythmic gymnastics	13.00 m	13.00 m	169 m²	14.00 m	14.00 m	196 m²	8.00 m	
Rugby	120.00 m	68.00 m	8,160 m²	125.00 m	73.00 m	9,125 m²		
Schlagball (rounders)	70.00 m	25.00 m	1,750 m²	80.00 m	45.00 m	3,600 m²		
Soccer (FIFA standard)	105.00 m	68.00 m	7,140 m²	120.00 m	80.00 m	9,600 m²	5.50 m	
Soccer, general	90.00–120.00 m	45.00–90.00 m	4,050–10,800 m²	94.00–124.00 m	47.00–92.00 m	4,418–11,408 m²	5.50 m	
Squash	9.75 m	6.40 m	63 m²	9.75 m	6.40 m	63 m²	2.13–4.57 m	
Table tennis	2.74 m	1.525 m	4.20 m²	14.00 m	7.00 m	98 m²	5.00 m	
Tennis	23.77 m	8.23–10.97 m	196–261 m²	36.57 m	18.27 m	669 m²	7.00 m	
Trampoline	7.57 m	3.03 m	23 m²	15.57 m	11.03 m	172 m²	8.00 m	
Ultimate Frisbee	109.73 m	36.58 m	4,014 m²	112.00 m	39.00 m	4,368 m²		
Volleyball	18.00 m	9.00 m	162 m²	24.00 m	15.00 m	360 m²	7.00 m	
Weightlifting	4.00 m	4.00 m	16 m²	10.00 m	10.00 m	100 m²	4.00 m	
Wrestling	9.00–12.00 m	9.00–12.00 m	81–144 m²	13.00–16.00 m	13.00–16.00 m	169–256 m²	4.00 m	
Wheel gymnastics	23.00 m	3.00 m	69 m²	27.00 m	15.00 m	405 m²	4.00 m	

Table 10.1 (continuation) Playing field sizes of various sports

Indoor soccer (Futsal)

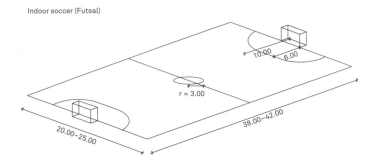

Soccer

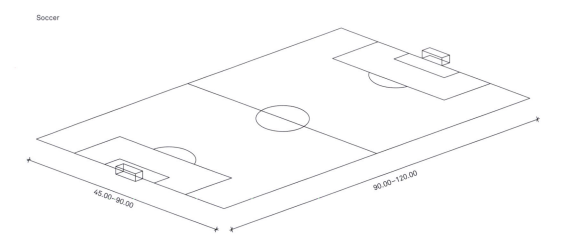

Soccer (as per FIFA standard)

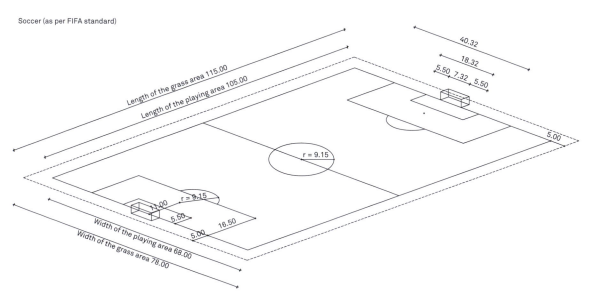

Figure 10.2 Playing field dimensions for soccer (association football)

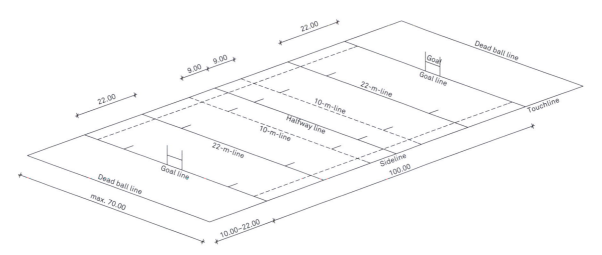

Figure 10.3 Playing field dimensions for rugby

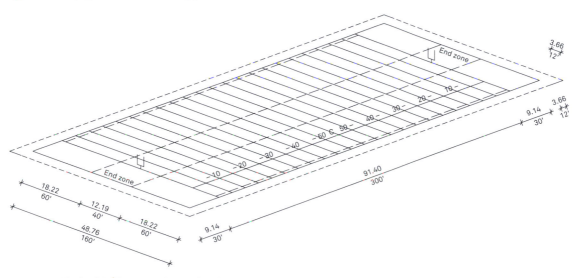

Figure 10.4 Playing field dimensions for American football

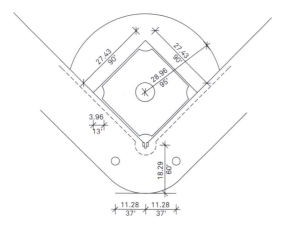

Figure 10.5 Baseball diamond

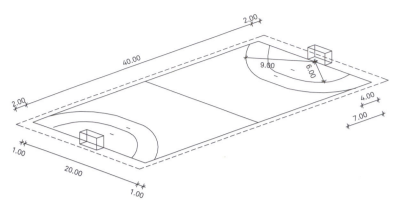

Figure 10.6 Court dimensions for handball

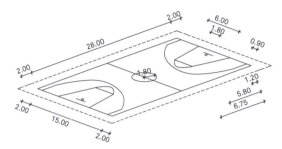

Figure 10.7 Court dimensions basketball

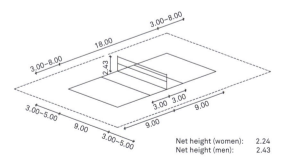

Net height (women): 2.24
Net height (men): 2.43

Figure 10.8 Court dimensions for volleyball

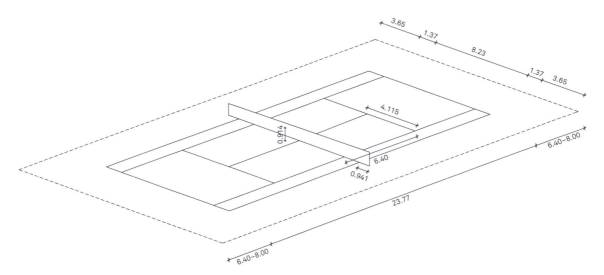

Figure 10.9 Court dimensions for tennis

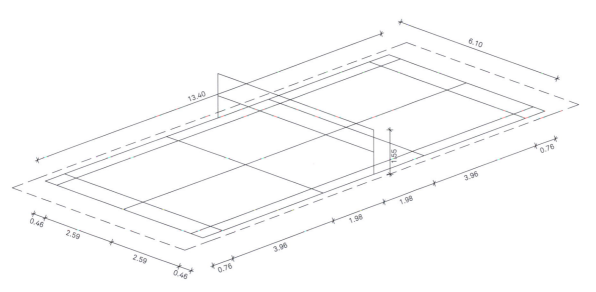

Figure 10.10 Court dimensions for badminton

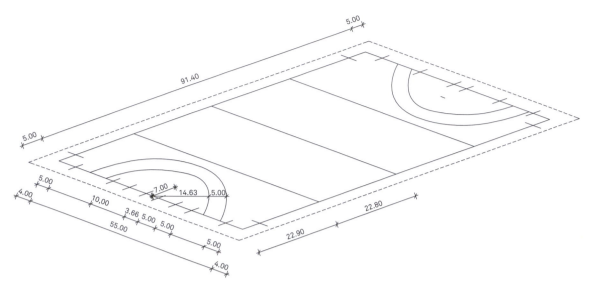

Figure 10.11　Playing field dimensions for field hockey

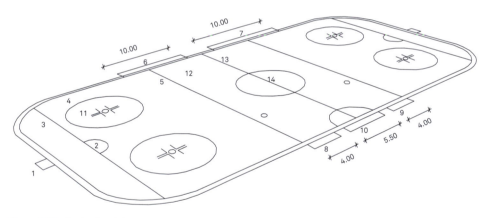

Figure 10.12　Ice hockey rink

1　Goal judge
2　Goal crease
3　Goal line, red, 0.05 m wide
4　Radius, 7.00 to 8.00 m
5　Blue line, 0.30 m wide
6　Players' bench, team A
7　Players' bench, team B
8　Penalty bench, team A
9　Penalty bench, team B
10　Scorekeeper's bench
11　End zone face-off spot and circle
12　Neutral zone face-off spot
13　Center line, red, 0.30 m wide
14　Center face-off spot and circle

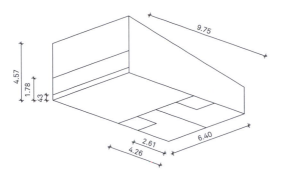

Figure 10.13   Court dimensions for squash

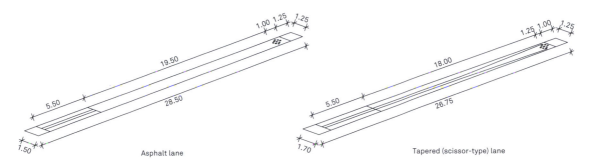

Asphalt lane

Tapered (scissor-type) lane

Figure 10.14   Lane dimensions for (ten-pin) bowling/nine-pin bowling

Pole vault

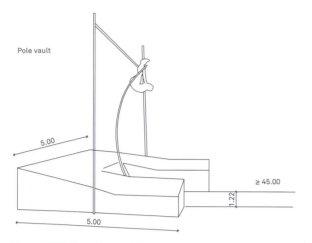

High jump

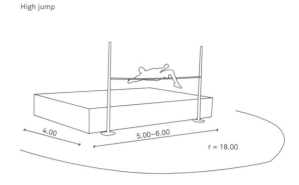

Figure 10.15 Dimensions for high jump and pole vault

Long jump

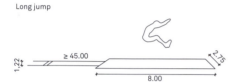

Triple jump

Figure 10.16 Dimensions for long jump and triple jump

Running track

Hurdle track

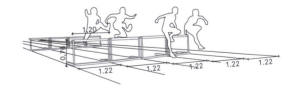

Figure 10.17 Dimensions for running tracks and hurdle tracks

Pool type	Water depth
Wading pool	max. 0.50/0.60 m
Nonswimmer pool	max. 1.35 m
Swimmer pool	min. 1.35 m, 1.80 m recommended
Water polo pool	min. 1.80 m, 2.00 m recommended
Olympic swimming pool	min. 2.00 m, 3.00 m recommended
Diving pool	min. 3.20 m, up to 4.50 m (depending on tower height)
Movable floor pools	Depth adjustable

Table 10.2 Water depths of swimming pools

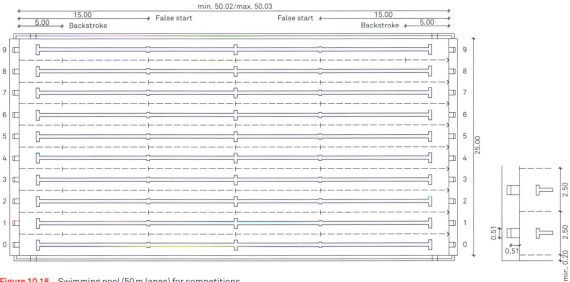

Figure 10.18 Swimming pool (50 m lanes) for competitions

Source: FINA

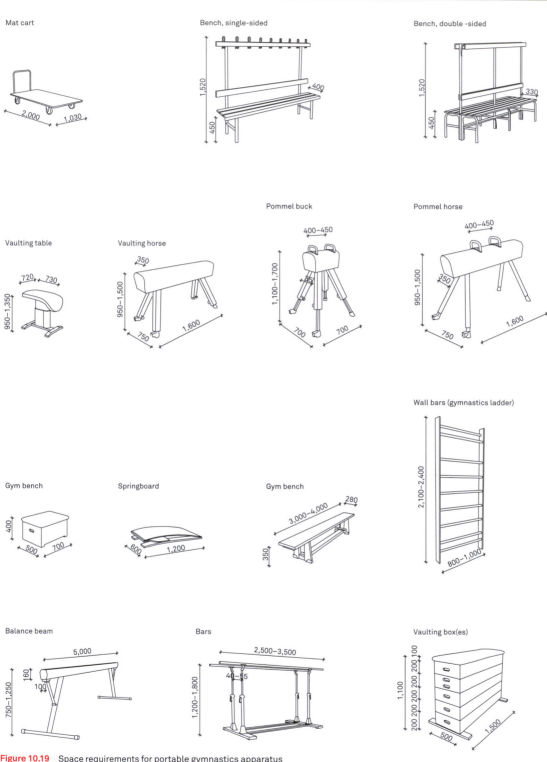

Figure 10.19 Space requirements for portable gymnastics apparatus

Apparatus	Obstacle-free zone				Safety clearance				Total area
	Length	Width	Height	Area	Lateral	Front	Rear	Side-by-side	
Floor performance area	14.00 m	14.00 m	4.50 m	196 m²					196 m²
Pommel horse	4.00 m	4.00 m	4.50 m	16 m²					16 m²
Vault	36.00 m	2.00 m	5.50 m	72 m²					72 m²
Rings (steady rings)	8.00 m	6.00 m	5.50 m	64 m²					64 m²
Bars	6.00 m	9.50 m	4.50 m	57 m²	2.00 m	4.00 m	3.00 m	4.50 m	176 m²
Horizontal bar (high bar)	12.00 m	6.00 m	7.00 m	72 m²	1.50 m	6.00 m	6.00 m		216 m²
Uneven bars	12.00 m	6.00 m	5.50 m	72 m²	1.50 m	6.00 m	6.00 m		216 m²
Balance beam	12.00 m	6.00 m	4.50 m	72 m²					72 m²
Flying rings	18.00 m	4.00 m	5.50 m	72 m²	1.50 m	10.50 m	7.50 m	1.50 m	252 m²
Climbing ropes					1.50 m	4.50 m	4.50 m	1.00 m	27 m²
Gymnastics wall bars						4.00 m	4.00 m	2.00 m	

Table 10.3 Space requirements for gymnastics apparatus

Raisable wall bars

Single and double section wall bars mounted within niches

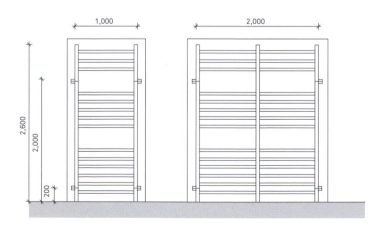

Figure 10.20 Space requirements for wall bars

Horizontal bar apparatus

Floor sleeve for horizontal bar

Horizontal bar, sinkable in floor

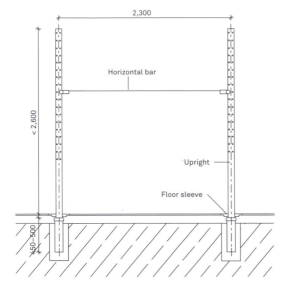

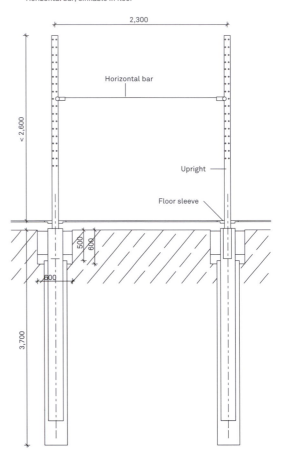

Figure 10.21 Space requirements for horizontal bars with removable and in-floor uprights

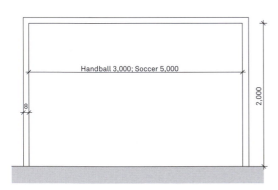

Figure 10.22 Goal for handball/indoor soccer, with anchorage

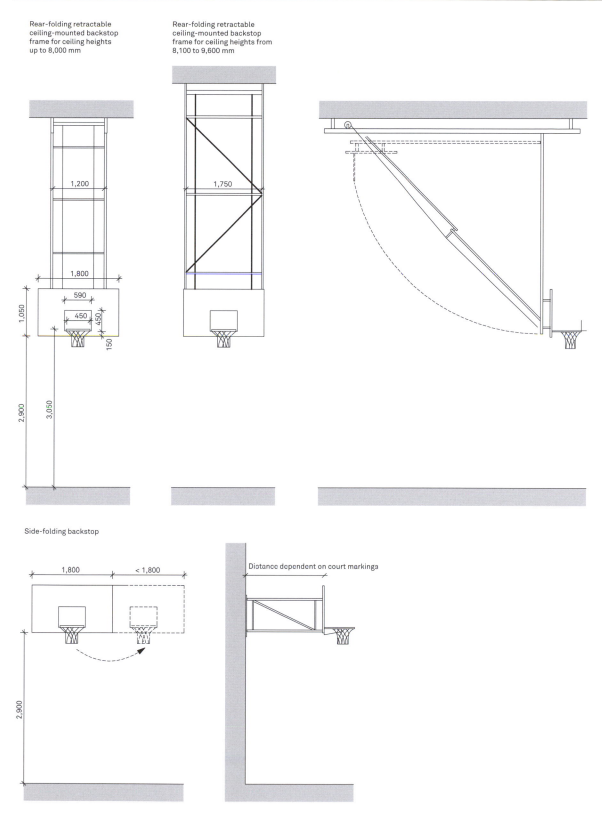

Rear-folding retractable ceiling-mounted backstop frame for ceiling heights up to 8,000 mm

Rear-folding retractable ceiling-mounted backstop frame for ceiling heights from 8,100 to 9,600 mm

Side-folding backstop

Distance dependent on court markings

Figure 10.23 Ceiling- and wall-mounted basketball backboards

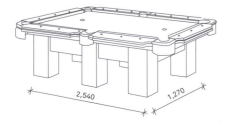

Billiards

Air hockey

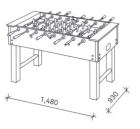

Foosball (table soccer)

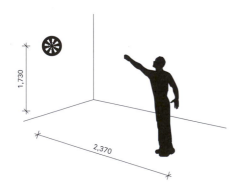

Darts

Figure 10.24 Various gaming tables

10.2 Tiered Seating and Spectator Areas

The planning of tiered seating must take account of the legal requirements for escape routes and the characteristics of various building parts as well as aspects of space efficiency and sight lines for good visibility of the playing area from all positions. In addition to determining the heights and angle of the tiered spectator seating, above all it is crucial to define the positions of the access points in such a way as to limit any lost seat positions and any restrictions on the spectators' lines of sight.

Seating positions can be along continuous benches or consist of individual seats. The minimum width of each seating position is 0.50 m, and the depth is about 0.35–0.40 m. The aisles must have a clear width of at least 0.40 m. For standing areas, crush barriers with a minimum height of 1.10 m must be provided.

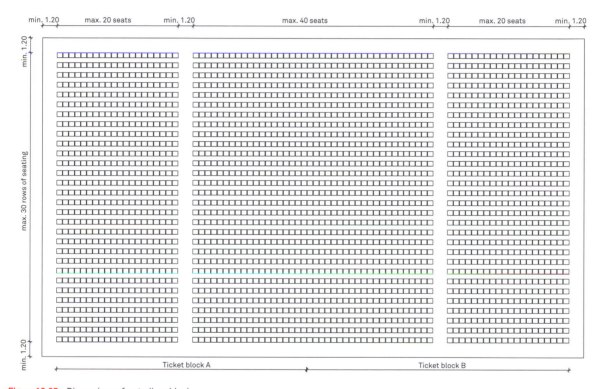

Figure 10.25 Dimensions of a stadium block

Source: VStättVO

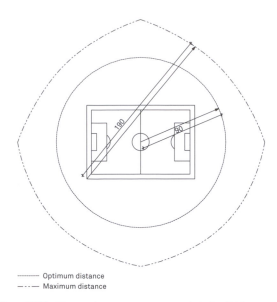

------- Optimum distance
—·— Maximum distance

Figure 10.26   Distance between spectators and playing field
As per FIFA

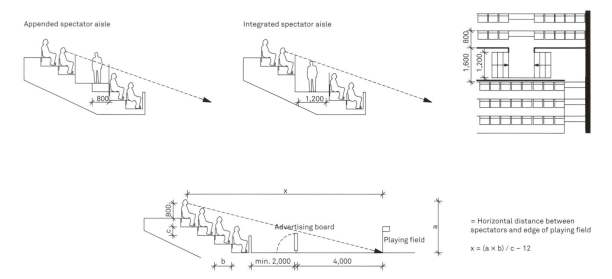

Figure 10.27   View of the playing field
Data source: FIFA: Football Stadiums – Technical Recommendations and Requirements

= Horizontal distance between spectators and edge of playing field

$$x = (a \times b) / c - 12$$

Minimum distances to avoid restricted sight lines

Fence or divider

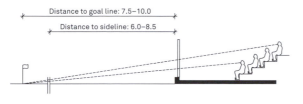

Trench

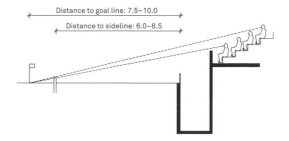

Raised tiered seating

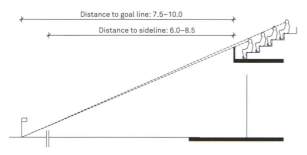

Figure 10.28 Options for excluding spectators from playing area without restricting sightlines

Source: FIFA

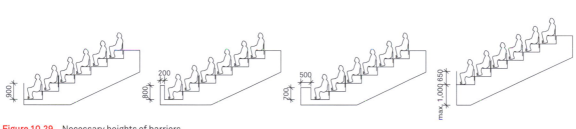

Figure 10.29 Necessary heights of barriers

Source: VStättVO

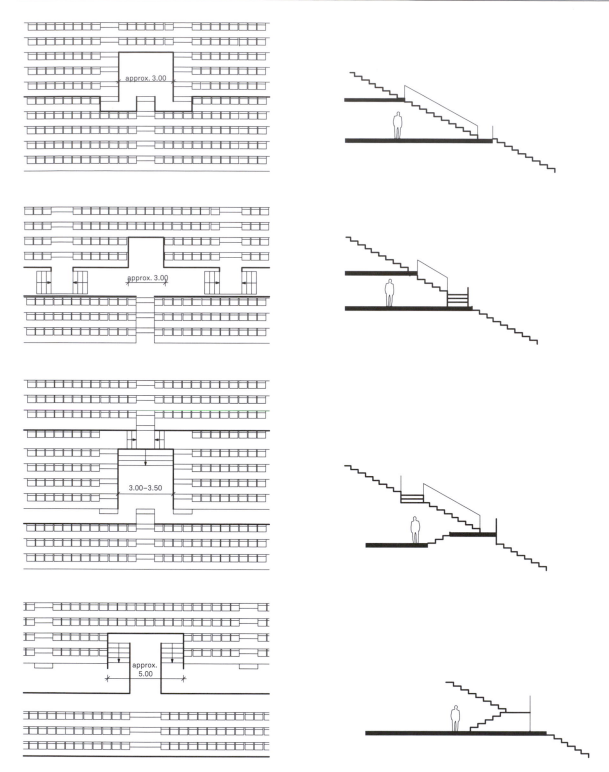

Figure 10.30   Access to stadium seating tiers

Folding seats

Fixed seats

Variable workplaces for journalists and commentators

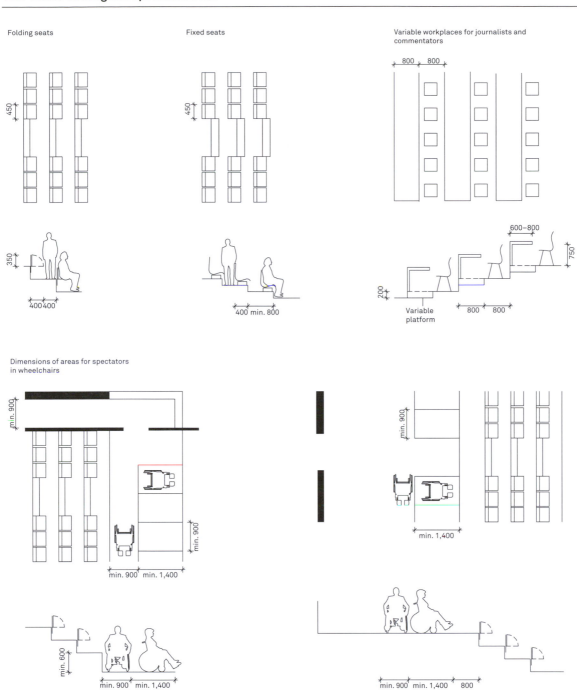

Dimensions of areas for spectators in wheelchairs

Figure 10.31 Arrangement of seats

Source: FIFA

10.3 Culture and Performing Arts

Museum and performing arts buildings are subdivided into one or more areas that are accessible to the public, which include the main exhibition and performance spaces and which usually do not require a direct relationship to the outside, and a non-public area that includes the necessary ancillary spaces and office workplaces that generally do require a connection to the outside.

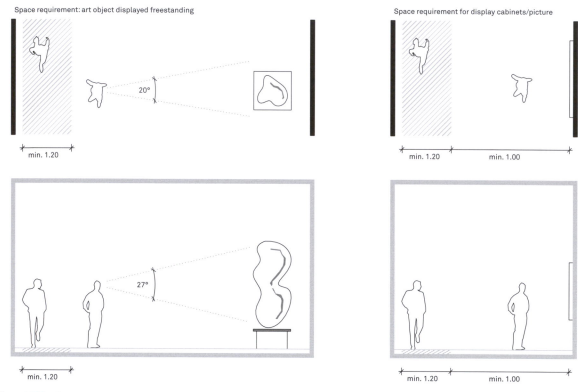

Space requirement: art object displayed freestanding

Space requirement for display cabinets/picture

Figure 10.32 Space requirement for exhibition objects

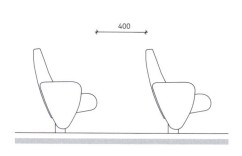

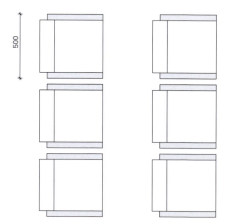

Figure 10.33 Rows of seating in performing arts buildings

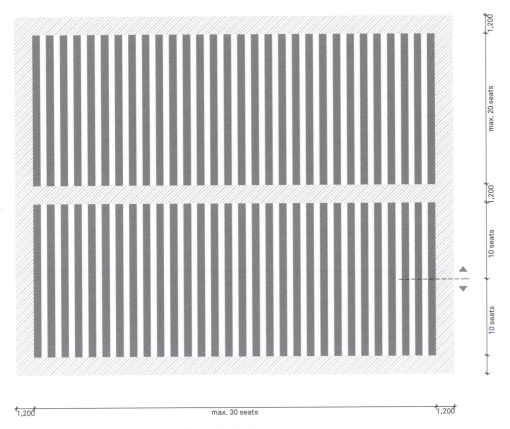

Figure 10.34 Maximum number of rows of seating in blocks

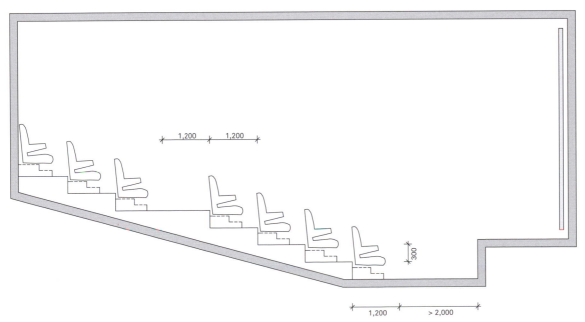

Figure 10.35 Cross section through a movie theater

11 Storage Spaces

Storage rooms must be incorporated when planning almost all types of buildings, although their type, size, and complexity can sometimes differ considerably. Very different terminology is used for the various types of storage, which are generally a consequence of the specific typology or the logistics concept. In addition to storing items in a spatially efficient way, the operation of storage areas is an important aspect when planning storage rooms, especially when, as in logistics buildings, storage of goods is an integral part of the business model.

11.1 Storerooms and Janitor's Closets

Storerooms and janitor's closets are needed in every building in sufficient number to enable care and technical maintenance of the building by cleaning personnel and custodial staff. Storerooms for maintaining supplies of small items such as replacement lamps, garden tools, etc., are expediently located in basement areas or near other technical plant areas. Cleaning supply rooms and janitor's closets may need to be established in multiple places within the building (usually close to plumbing cores) in order to avoid long distances. At a minimum, a janitor's closet should contain a janitor's sink with running water, floor space for cleaning equipment, and a shelf for cleaning materials.

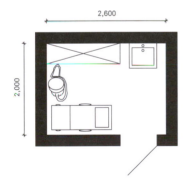

Figure 11.1 Janitor's closet

Figure 11.2 Cleaning cart

11.2 Pallets and Containers

Dependent on the various sizes of items being stored, different standardized systems for transporting and storing these goods with ease and efficiency have become established. The storage room or storage building must be dimensioned accordingly. In addition to disposable packaging/pallets, reusable elements such as Euro pallets, big bags (also known as bulk bags or flexible intermediate bulk containers [FIBC]), intermediate bulk containers (IPC, also known as IBC totes or pallet tanks) and ISO freight containers are used. Many warehouses are therefore specifically coordinated with the standardized 800 × 1,200 mm pallet systems as well as the 20- and 40-foot ISO containers.

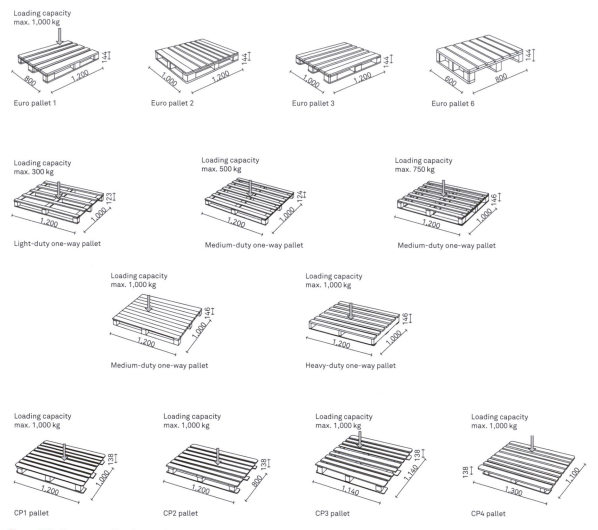

Figure 11.3 Transport pallets for warehouses

Metal collars for
flat pallets

Pallet-mounted frame
with safety retainers

Metal stacking frame

Middle clamping bracket
for Euro pallet

Wood collars for
Euro/flat pallets

Flat pallet with collar

Clamping brackets
with mesh dividers

Pallets for full and
half warp beams or
back beams

Box pallet with lid and
removable side panel

Attachable pipe
frames

Flat pallet with
stacking frame

Partitionable mesh
box pallet

Large-capacity or
insulation pallet

2-piece collapsible
pallet converter

Figure 11.4 Various types of transport devices

Intermediate Bulk Container IBC

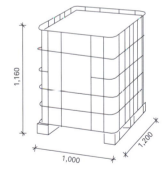

1,160
1,200
1,000

Small load carrier

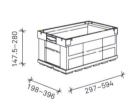

147.5–280
198–396 297–594

Large load carrier

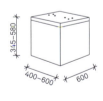

530–975
600–1,000 800–1,200

Polystyrene boxes

345–580
400–600 600

Figure 11.5 Various storage containers

Type	Outer dimensions (L × W × H)	Inner dimensions (L × W × H)	Volume	Empty weight (tare)	Max. capacity	Max. total weight
20-foot	6.058 × 2.438 × 2.591 m 19' 10½" × 8' × 8' 6"	5.710 × 2.352 × 2.385 m 18' 8¹³⁄₁₆" × 7' 8¹⁹⁄₃₂" × 7' 9⁵⁷⁄₆₄"	33.0 m³	2,250 kg	21,750 kg	24,000 kg
40-foot	12.192 × 2.438 × 2.591 m 40' × 8' × 8' 6"	12.040 × 2.345 × 2.385 m 39' 5⁴⁵⁄₆₄" × 7' 8¹⁹⁄₃₂" × 7' 9⁵⁷⁄₆₄"	67.0 m³	3,780 kg	26,700 kg	30,480 kg
40-foot high cube	12.192 × 2.438 × 2.896 m 40' × 8' × 9' 6"	12.040 × 2.345 × 2.690 m 39' 4" × 7' 7" × 8' 9"	76.0 m³	3,900 kg	26,580 kg	30,480 kg
45-foot high cube	13.716 × 2.438 × 2.896 m 45' × 8' × 9' 6"	13.556 × 2.345 × 2.695 m 44' 4" × 7' 8¹⁹⁄₃₂" × 8' 9¹⁵⁄₁₆"	86.0 m³	5,050 kg	27,450 kg	32,500 kg
53-foot high cube	16.154 × 2.591 × 2.896 m 53' × 8' 6" × 9' 6"	16.002 × 2.515 × 2.710 m 52' 6" × 8' 3" × 8' 10¹¹⁄₁₆"	109.1 m³			

Table 11.1   Dimensions of ISO containers (selection)

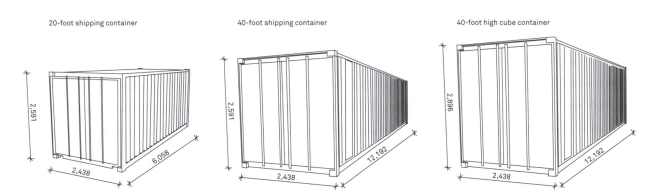

20-foot shipping container   40-foot shipping container   40-foot high cube container

Figure 11.6   ISO containers

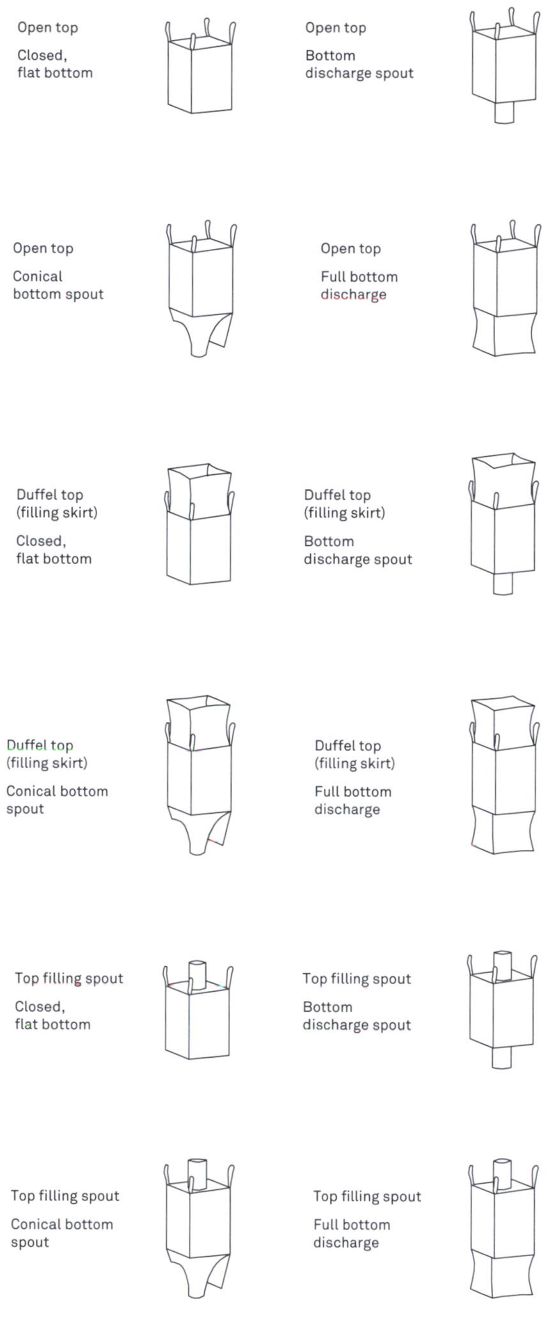

Open top
Closed,
flat bottom

Open top
Bottom
discharge spout

Open top
Conical
bottom spout

Open top
Full bottom
discharge

Duffel top
(filling skirt)
Closed,
flat bottom

Duffel top
(filling skirt)
Bottom
discharge spout

Duffel top
(filling skirt)
Conical bottom
spout

Duffel top
(filling skirt)
Full bottom
discharge

Top filling spout
Closed,
flat bottom

Top filling spout
Bottom
discharge spout

Top filling spout
Conical bottom
spout

Top filling spout
Full bottom
discharge

Figure 11.7 Typical big bags (FIBC)

Big Bag			
Type: Standard 4-loop container			
Measurements	Various footprint sizes		
Inner dimensions	760 × 760 mm	870 × 870 mm	950 × 950 mm
Outer dimensions	800 × 800 mm	910 × 910 mm	990 × 990 mm
Diameter of big bag, filled	1,010 mm	1,150 mm	1,250 mm
Volume (m³)	**Height (mm)**		
0.3	550	–	–
0.4	650	–	–
0.5	800	650	–
0.6	900	750	–
0.7	1,050	850	–
0.8	1,150	950	–
0.9	1,250	1,050	850
1	1,400	1,150	950
1.1	1,550	1,250	1,050
1.2	1,650	1,350	1,150
1.3	1,800	1,450	1,200
1.4	1,900	1,550	1,300
1.5	–	1,650	1,350
1.6	–	1,750	1,450
1.7	–	1,850	1,550
1.8	–	1,950	1,600
1.9	–	2,050	1,700
2	–	2,150	1,750
2.1	–	–	1,850
2.2	–	–	1,950

11.3 Types of Storage

The type of storage needed depends on the requirements of the items being stored, the availability, the stored diversity of goods, etc. A basic distinction is made between static vs. dynamic or chaotic storage systems, which are subject to automated processes. Both systems can be organized as compact storage or line storage, and whereas compact storage offers more efficient use of space, line storage enables access to all the stored goods. Further distinctions are made based on the storage height and the loading capacity (for example, high-rise rack, heavy-duty rack) or specific properties, such as storage systems utilizing mobile carousels, paternosters, rolling racks, or mobile shelving.

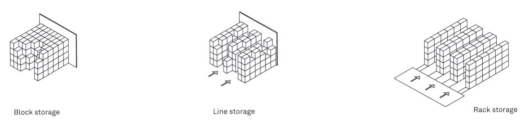

Block storage   Line storage   Rack storage

Figure 11.8   Block, line, and rack storage

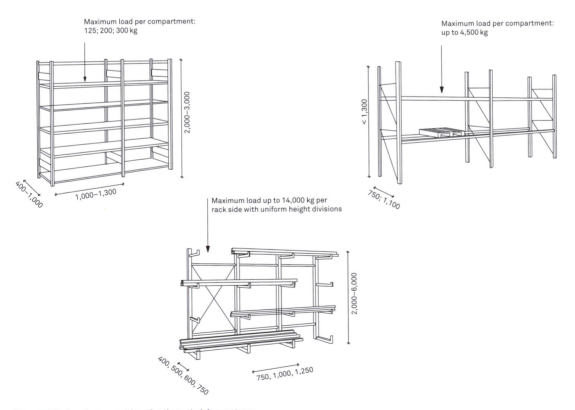

Figure 11.9   Loading capacities of various shelving systems

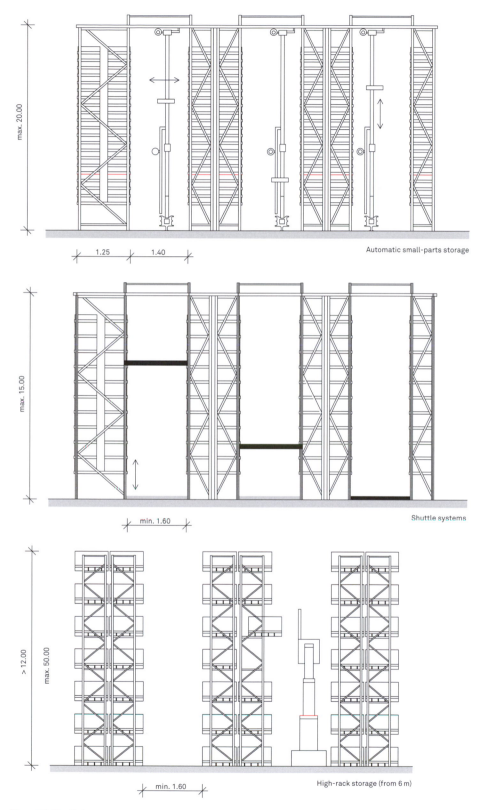

max. 20.00

1.25   1.40

Automatic small-parts storage

max. 15.00

min. 1.60

Shuttle systems

> 12.00

max. 50.00

min. 1.60

High-rack storage (from 6 m)

Figure 11.10 High-rack storage systems

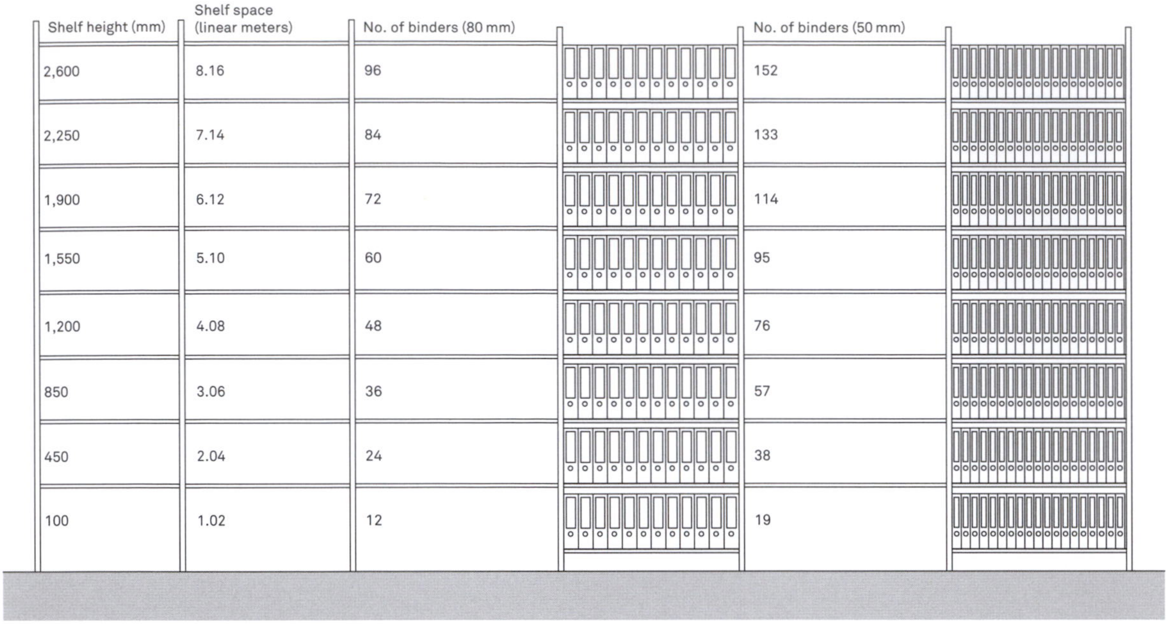

Shelf height (mm)	Shelf space (linear meters)	No. of binders (80 mm)		No. of binders (50 mm)	
2,600	8.16	96		152	
2,250	7.14	84		133	
1,900	6.12	72		114	
1,550	5.10	60		95	
1,200	4.08	48		76	
850	3.06	36		57	
450	2.04	24		38	
100	1.02	12		19	

Figure 11.11 Binder storage in filing shelves

11.4 Handling and Transport

When planning storage areas, adequate circulation routes and maneuvering areas are to be incorporated for loading and unloading. A decisive factor in this respect is whether operations shall be automated or carried out manually, since automated rack-serving equipment generally requires less space than human-operated ground conveyors like pallet trucks or forklifts. In addition to accommodating the actual warehouse operations, consideration must also be given to the transfer areas, including turning areas, crossing vehicle paths, gates, etc. For automated warehouses, warehouse management systems must be used to provide appropriate areas for stocking and picking as well as packing and shipping stations.

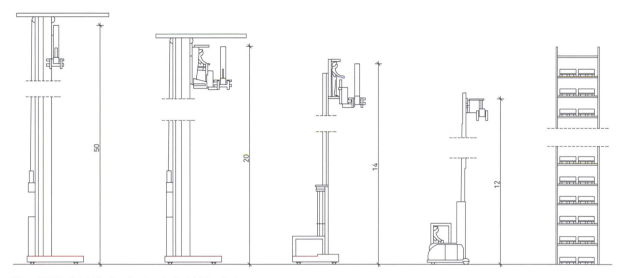

Figure 11.12 Height limits of various industrial trucks in m

Vehicle			Outside turning radius of wheels	Remarks	Clear height above traffic routes	
Type	Width	Length			Trucks with no or low lift height (max. 1,200 mm lift)	High-lift trucks
Pedestrian-controlled industrial trucks (walkies)	800–1,300	1,200–2,000	1,000–1,600		2,000	3,500
Stand-up rider trucks	900–1,500	1,500–2,500	1,500–2,000		2,500	3,500
Sit-down rider trucks	900–1,500	2,500–3,800	1,500–2,500	Dimensions apply only to forklifts with a carrying capacity of max. 3 t	2,500	3,500
Mobile cranes	1,500–2,500	3,500–5,500	2,500–7,200	For mobile cranes with max. 9 t carrying capacity	4,000	4,000
Light trucks with max. 1.5 t loading capacity	1,500–2,400	4,000–5,000	4,000–6,000	For trucks with 6000 mm vehicle length	4,000	4,000

Table 11.2 Space requirements of conveyor vehicles in mm
Per ASR A1.8

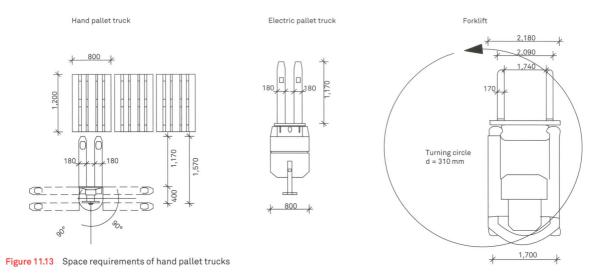

Figure 11.13 Space requirements of hand pallet trucks

Type of lifting device	AST (minimum aisle width)	Number of storage	Number of pallets per m²
Forklift	2,300 mm	4 levels	1.8
Counterbalance truck	4,000 mm	4 levels	1.6
		6 levels	2.2
Pallet stacker	2,300 mm	4 levels	1.8
		6 levels	2.7
Pallet stacker with telescopic fork	2,400 mm	4 levels	1.7
		6 levels	2.6
Reach mast truck	1,000 mm	4 levels	1.7
		6 levels	2.5
		8 levels	3.2
High rack stacker with swivel traverse fork	1,000 mm	4 levels	2.0
		6 levels	2.9
		8 levels	4.1
		10 levels	5.2
High-rack storage with telescopic platform	1,500 mm	4 levels	2.2
		6 levels	3.2
		8 levels	4.3
		10 levels	5.4

Table 11.3 Quantity of pallets as a function of lifting device type

Belt conveyor

Wheel conveyor

Gravity roller conveyor

Drag chain conveyor

Slat-band chain conveyor

Mesh belt conveyor

Scraper conveyor

Pallet belt conveyor

Figure 11.14   Types of conveyors in mm

12 Technical Equipment Rooms

Building services installations are an integral part of a functioning and effective overall concept. Due to increasing requirements for energy efficiency and growing capabilities for networking and controllability of building services, the interdependencies of building parts and system components are becoming ever more complex. Thus the connections to public utility networks, the installation area for building services components such as boilers and ventilation systems, data networks, server equipment, etc., as well as the distribution of the utilities within the building is best planned from the outset.

12.1 Connections to Public Utilities

The supply mains for water, electricity, gas, communication media, etc., and the sewer mains are typically all within the confines of the public right-of-way. The handover point is located either at the property line, in a manhole, or in the service connection room within the building. When laying out utility connections, different minimum installation depths must be observed in some cases. For sewer lines in particular, the pipe connection heights at the street and the height of the backflow level must be taken into account.

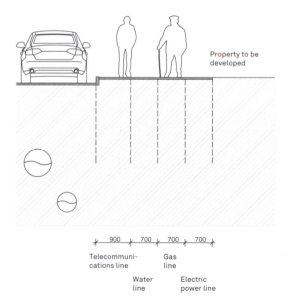

Figure 12.1 Positions of utility lines beneath public right-of-way

Type of utility line	Depth under t.o. grade
Telecommunications line	350–600 mm
Water line	1,200–1,500 mm
Gas line	500–1,000 mm
Electric power line	600–800 mm
District heating	600–1,000 mm

Table 12.1 Installation depths of utility lines

12.2 Mains Connection Rooms and Meter Rooms

The service connection room, or meter room, is where the interface is made between the supply to the building and the building's internal networks. Whenever possible, meter rooms should be located on the ground floor or in the basement, directly along the exterior wall and facing toward a public street. Depending on the building size and type, meter rooms must be ventilated and enclosed by fire-rated walls. It may be necessary to provide separate rooms for different utilities, so the planner must make allowances for such areas early in the design. In general, utilities such as heating are either distributed in the basement and fed along multiple vertical risers to the points of use or routed along a central shaft supplying all the sto-

ries, with distribution and shut-off/metering possibilities at each floor. Depending on the system chosen, space for shafts and/or distribution rooms must be included in the plans at an early stage. In some cases accessible shafts are also used for locating shut-off valves and distribution points, and in other cases separate distribution cabinets/rooms are located near the shafts. For reasons of fire safety, either the shaft itself is compartmentalized with firestops at each floor level or firestops are used at each point of exit into the individual stories. In both cases, the planner must include adequate installation space for firestopping and fire dampers (in the dimensioning of suspended ceiling plenums, for example).

Without district heating connection	Max. 30 dwelling units	Max. 60 dwelling units
With district heating connection	Max. 10 dwelling units	Max. 30 dwelling units
Depth	> 2.00 m	> 2.00 m
Width	> 1.80 m	> 3.50 m
Height	> 2.00 m	> 2.00 m

Table 12.2 Service connection room for residential buildings

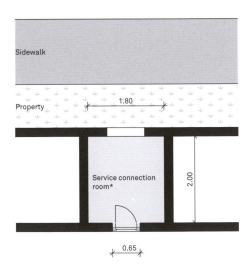

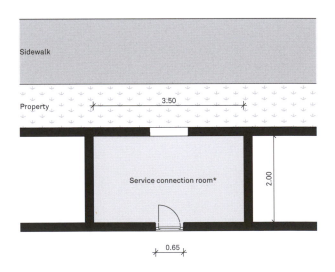

* Service connection room for up to approximately 30 dwelling units (up to approximately 10 dwelling units with district heating)

* Service connection room for up to approximately 60 dwelling units (up to approximately 30 dwelling units with district heating)

Figure 12.2 Service connection room for residential buildings

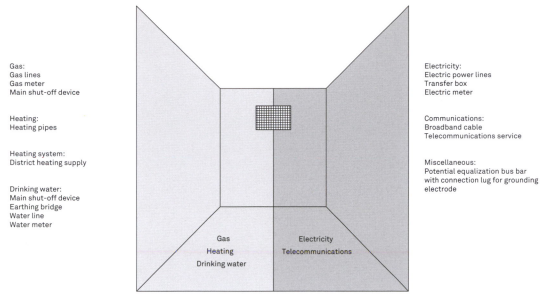

Gas:
Gas lines
Gas meter
Main shut-off device

Heating:
Heating pipes

Heating system:
District heating supply

Drinking water:
Main shut-off device
Earthing bridge
Water line
Water meter

Electricity:
Electric power lines
Transfer box
Electric meter

Communications:
Broadband cable
Telecommunications service

Miscellaneous:
Potential equalization bus bar
with connection lug for grounding
electrode

Gas
Heating
Drinking water

Electricity
Telecommunications

Figure 12.3   Elements within the service connection room

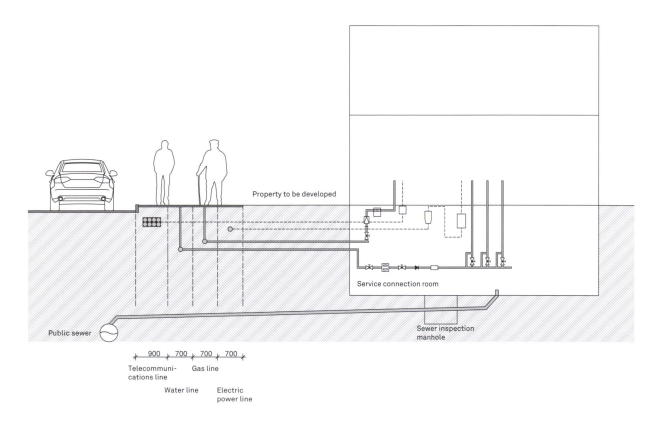

Property to be developed

Service connection room

Public sewer

Sewer inspection
manhole

900   700   700   700

Telecommuni-
cations line

Gas line

Water line

Electric
power line

Figure 12.4   Vertical section through the utility connections

Literature

General References

American Institute of Architects. *Architectural Graphic Standards*, 12th ed. Hoboken: Wiley, 2006.

American Planning Association (APA). *Planning and Urban Design Standards*. Hoboken: Wiley, 2006.

Bielefeld, Bert, ed. *Planning Architecture. Dimensions and Typologies.* Basel: Birkhäuser, 2016

Bielefeld, Bert, and Isabella Skiba. *Basics Technical Drawing*, 2nd rev. ed. Basel: Birkhäuser, 2013.

Ching, Francis D. K., and Steven R. Winkel. *Building Codes Illustrated: A Guide to Understanding the International Building Code*, 4th ed. Hoboken: Wiley, 2012.

De Chiara, Joseph, and Mike Crosbie. *Time-Saver Standards for Building Types*, 4th ed. New York: McGraw-Hill, 2001.

De Chiara, Joseph, Julius Panero, and Martin Zelnik. *Time-Saver Standards for Interior Design and Space Planning*, 2nd ed. New York: McGraw-Hill, 2001.

Deplazes, Andrea, ed. *Constructing Architecture: Materials, Processes, Structures*, 3rd ed. Basel: Birkhäuser, 2013.

Harmon, Sharon K., and Katherine E. Kennon. *The Codes Guidebook for Interiors*, 6th ed. Hoboken: Wiley, 2014.

Harris, Charles, and Nicholas Dines. *Time-Saver Standards for Landscape Architecture: Design and Construction Data*, 2nd ed. New York: McGraw-Hill, 1998.

Heiss, Oliver, Christine Degenhart, and Johann Ebe. *Barrier-Free Design: Principles, Planning, Examples*, translated by Gerd H. Söffker and Philip Thrift. Edition Detail. Basel: Birkhäuser, 2010.

International Code Council: *International Building Code*, 2015 edition, ICC/Cengage Learning, Clifton Park, NY 2014. The 2012 edition is available online at http://publicecodes.cyberregs.com/icod/, last accessed June 11, 2016.

Littlefield, David, ed. *Metric Handbook: Planning and Design Data*. 4th ed. New York: Routledge, 2012.

Neufert, Ernst, and Peter Neufert. *Architect's Data*, 4th ed., updated by Johannes Kister et al., translated by David Sturge. Chichester: Wiley-Blackwell, 2012.

Watson, Donald, and Michael J. Crosbie, eds. *Time-Saver Standards for Architectural Design: Technical Data for Professional Practice*, 8th ed. New York: McGraw-Hill, 2004.

Zimmermann, Astrid, ed. *Constructing Landscape: Materials, Techniques, Structural Components*, 3rd ed. Basel: Birkhäuser, 2015.

Zimmermann, Astrid. *Planning Landscape: Dimensions, Elements, Typologies*. Basel: Birkhäuser, 2015.

Chapter 2: Human Measure

Bogardus, Emory S. "Measuring Social Distances," *Journal of Applied Sociology* 9 (1925): 299–308.

Bundesministerium für Gesundheit. *Handbuch für Planer und Praktiker*. Bad Homburg, 1996.

Flügel, Bernd, Holle Greil, and Karl Sommer. *Anthropologischer Atlas*. Frankfurt am Main: Wötzel, 1986.

Gehl, Jan. *Life Between Buildings: Using Public Space*, rev. ed., translated by Jo Koch. New York: Van Nostrand Reinhold, 1987. Originally published as Livet mellem husene (1971).

Hall, Edward T. *The Hidden Dimension*. Garden City, NY: Doubleday, 1966.

Jürgens, Hans, Ivar Aune, and Ursula Pieper. *International Data on Anthropometry*. Geneva: International Labour Office, 1990.

Le Corbusier. *The Modulor and Modulor 2*. Basel: Birkhäuser, 2000.

Panero, Julius, and Martin Zelnik. *Human Dimension & Interior Space: A Source Book of Design Reference Standards*. New York: Whitney Library of Design, 1979.

Pheasant, Stephen. *Bodyspace: Anthropometry, Ergonomics and the Design of Work*. London: Taylor & Francis Ltd, 2005.

Skiba, Isabella, and Rahel Züger. *Basics Barrier-Free Planning*. Basel: Birkhäuser, 2009.

Stolzenberg, H., H. Kahl, and K. E. Bergmann. "Körpermaße bei Kindern und Jugendlichen in Deutschland," *Bundesgesundheitsblatt – Gesundheitsforschung – Gesundheitsschutz* 50, no. 5–6 (2007): 659–69.

Chapter 3: Exterior Spaces

Auhagen, Axel, Klaus Ermer, and Rita Mohrmann. *Landschaftsplanung in der Praxis*. Stuttgart: Ulmer, 2002.

Booth, Norman K. *Basic Elements of Landscape Architectural Design*. Long Grove, IL: Waveland Press, 1990.

Kirchhoff, Peter. *Städtische Verkehrsplanung: Konzepte, Verfahren, Maßnahmen*. Wiesbaden: Vieweg+Teubner, 2002.

Köhler, Uwe. *Einführung in die Verkehrsplanung*. Stuttgart: Fraunhofer IRB, 2014.

Lohse, Dieter. *Verkehrsplanung*, 3rd ed. Berlin: Beuth, 2011.

Weidinger, Jürgen, eds. *Atmosphären Entwerfen*. Berlin: TU Berlin, 2014.

Weiland, Ulrike. *Einführung in die Raum- und Umweltplanung*. Stuttgart: UTB, 2007.

Chapter 4: Interior Circulation

Schittich, Christian, ed. *Designing Circulation Areas, Staged Paths and Innovative Floorplan Concepts*. Berlin: Edition Detail, 2013.

Chapter 5: Living and Sleeping Spaces

Ebner, Peter, et al. *typology+. Innovative Residential Architecture*. Basel: Birkhäuser, 2009.

Feddersen, Eckhard, and Insa Lüdtke. *Living for the Elderly*. Basel: Birkhäuser, 2010.

Gast, Klaus-Peter. *Living Plans: New Concepts for Advanced Housing*. Basel: Birkhäuser, 2005.

Heckmann, Oliver, and Friederike Schneider. *Floor Plan Manual: Housing*, 4th ed. Basel: Birkhäuser, 2011.

Heisel, Joachim. *Planungsatlas: Das kompakte Planungsbuch für den Bauentwurf mit Projektbeispielen*, 4th ed. Berlin: Beuth, 2004.

Huber, Andreas, ed. *New Approaches to Housing for the Second Half of Life*. Basel: Birkhäuser, 2008.

Knirsch, Jürgen. *Hotels: Planen und Gestalten*, 4th ed. Leinfelden-Echterdingen: Knoch, 2001.

König, Roland. *Leitfaden barrierefreier Wohnungsbau*, 3rd ed. Stuttgart: Fraunhofer IRB, 2005.

Krebs, Jan. *Basics Design and Living*. Basel: Birkhäuser, 2007.

Lawson, Fred. *Hotels and Resorts: Planning, Design and Refurbishment*. Oxford: Butterworth Architecture, 1995.

Leupen, Bernard, and Harald Mooij. *Housing Design: A Manual*, 2nd ed. Rotterdam: nai010, 2012.

Miller, Richard. *Casino & Hotel Design Guidelines*. Charleston, SC: CreateSpace, 2012.

Perkins, Bradford, and J. David Hoglund. *Building Type Basics for Senior Living*, 2nd ed. Hoboken: Wiley, 2010.

Ronstedt, Manfred, and Tobias Frey. *Hotel Buildings: Construction and Design Manual*. Berlin: DOM Publishers, 2014.

Rutes, Walter, and Richard Penner. *Hotel Planning and Design*. New York: Architectural Press, 1985.

Schneider, Friederike, and Oliver Heckmann. *Floor Plan Manual: Housing*, 4th ed. Basel: Birkhäuser, 2011.

Skiba, Isabella, and Rahel Züger. *Basics Barrier-Free Planning*. Basel: Birkhäuser, 2009.

Stamm-Teske, Walter, et al. *Raumpilot Wohnen*. Stuttgart: Krämer, 2010.

Wietzorrek, Ulrike. *Housing+*. Basel: Birkhäuser, 2014.

Chapter 6: Kitchens and Dining Areas

Aicher, Otl. *Die Küche zum Kochen: Werkstatt einer neuen Lebenskultur*, 3rd ed. Staufen bei Freiburg: Ökobuch, 2005.

Ausschuss für staatlichen Hochbau, Bauministerkonferenz. *Planung und Bau von Küchen und Kantinen für 50 bis 1000 Verpflegungsteilnehmer*. Hanover: HIS Hochschul-Informations-System, 2002. Available online: https://www.is-argebau.de/Dokumente/4231417.pdf

Baraban, Regina S., and Joseph F. Durocher. *Successful Restaurant Design*, 3rd ed. Hoboken: Wiley, 2010.

Birchfield, John C. *Design and Layout of Foodservice Facilities*, 3rd ed. Hoboken: Wiley, 2007.

Loeschke, Gerhard, and Jutta Höfs. *Großküchen*. Wiesbaden: Bauverlag, 1985.

Noever, Peter, ed. *Die Frankfurter Küche von Margarete Schütte-Lihotzky: die Frankfurter Küche aus der Sammlung des MAK – Österreichisches Museum für Angewandte Kunst, Wien*. Berlin: Ernst & Sohn, 1992.

Chapter 7: Sanitary Facilities and Ancillary Rooms

Feurich, Hugo. *Grundlagen der Sanitärtechnik, Sanitärräume, Sanitäreinrichtung, Krankenhauseinrichtungen, physikalische Therapie-Einrichtungen, Wasserversorgung*, 10th exp. ed. Düsseldorf: Krammer, 2011.

Gause, Jo Allen, et al. *Office Development Handbook*, 2nd ed. Washington, DC: Urban Land Institute, 1998.

Kramer, Klaus. *Das private Hausbad 1850–1950*. Schiltach: Hansgrohe, 1997.

Pistohl, Wolfram, Christian Rechenauer, and Birgit Scheuerer. *Handbuch der Gebäudetechnik, vol. 1, Planungsgrundlagen und Beispiele*, 8th ed. Cologne: Werner, 2013.

Wellpott, Edwin, and Dirk Bohne. *Technischer Ausbau von Gebäuden*, 9th rev. and upd. ed., Stuttgart: Kohlhammer, 2006.

Chapter 8: Work Environments

Clements-Croome, Derek. *Creating the Productive Workplace*. New York: Taylor & Francis, 2006.

Hascher, Rainer, Simone Jeska, Thomas Arnold, and Birgit Klauck. *Office Buildings. A Design Manual*. Basel: Birkhäuser, 2002.

Institut für Internationale Architektur-Dokumentation, ed. *Büro/ Office*. Munich: Detail, 2013.

Kohn, A. Eugene, and Paul Katz. *Building Type Basics for Office Buildings*. Hoboken: Wiley, 2002.

Marmot, Alexi, and Joanna Eley. *Office Space Planning: Designs for Tomorrow's Workspace*. New York: McGraw Hill, 2000.

Streit, Wilhelm, and Ernst-Friedrich Pernack, eds. *Arbeitsstätten*, 8th ed. Heidelberg: ecomed Sicherheit, 2011.

Chapter 9: Communication and Education Spaces

Appleton, Ian. *Buildings for the Performing Arts: A Design and Development Guide*, 2nd ed. Oxford: Elsevier, 2008.

Armstrong, Leslie, and Roger Morgan. *Space for Dance: An Architectural Design Guide*. New York: Publishing Center for Cultural Resources, 1984.

Barron, Michael. *Auditorium Acoustics and Architectural Design*. London: Spon Press, 2009.

Cavanaugh, William J., Gregory C. Tocci, and Joseph A. Wilkes. *Architectural Acoustics: Principles and Practice*. Hoboken: Wiley, 2010.

Hardy, Hugh, and Stephen A. Kliment. *Building Type Basics for Performing Arts Facilities*. Hoboken: Wiley, 2006.

Lawson, Fred. *Congress, Convention and Exhibition Facilities: Planning, Design and Management*. Architectural Press Planning and Design Series. Oxford: Architectural, 2000.

Lederer, Arno, Barbara Pampe, and Wüstenrot Stiftung, eds. *Raumpilot Lernen*. Stuttgart: Krämer, 2012.

Long, Marshall. *Architectural Acoustics*. Boston: Elsevier, 2014.

Schittich, Christian, ed. *In Detail: Exhibitions and Displays*. Basel: Birkhäuser, 2009.

Sheard, Rod, and Christopher Lee. *Sports Buildings: A Design Manual*. Basel: Birkhäuser, 2016.

Steele, James. *Museum Builders*. London: Academy Editions, 1994.

—. *Theatre Builders: A Collaborative Art*. London: Academy Editions, 1996.

Strong, Judith. *Theatre Buildings: A Design Guide*. Abingdon: Routledge, 2010.

von Naredi-Rainer, Paul. *Museum Buildings: A Design Manual*. Basel: Birkhäuser, 2004.

Stürzebecher, Peter, and Sigrid Ulrich. *Architecture for Sport, New Concepts and International Projects for Sport and Leisure*, translated by Cybertechnics and Lucy Isenberg. Chichester: Wiley-Academy, 2001.

Vandenberg, M. *Stadium Builders*, Wiley-Academy.

van Uffelen, Chris. *Stadiums and Arenas: The Architecture of Games. Architecture for Fun, Sports and Leisure*. Salenstein: Braun, 2009.

Chapter 10: Sports and Recreation Facilities

Deutscher Schwimm-Verband e.V. *Bau- und Ausstattungsanforderungen für wettkampfgerechte Schwimmsportstätten*. 2012.

Diedrich, Richard J. *Building Type Basics for Recreational Facilities*. Hoboken: Wiley, 2005.

Forschungsgesellschaft Landschaftsentwicklung Landschaftsbau (FLL), in cooperation with the Deutsche Reiterliche Vereinigung (FN). *Empfehlungen für Planung, Bau und Instandhaltung von Reitplätzen*. 2014.

John, Geraint, Rod Sheard, and Ben Vickerey. *Stadia: The Populous Design and Development Guide*. London: Routledge, 2013.

Koordinierungskreis Bader. *Richtlinien für den Bäderbau*. KOK-Richtlinien. 2013.

Krämer, Thomas. *Outdoor Sportstätten: Ratgeber Planung & Bau*. Brühl: Stadionwelt, 2013.

Mackintosh, Iain. *Architecture, Actor and Audience. Theatre Concepts*. London: Routledge, 2003.

Nixdorf, Stefan. *StadiumATLAS: Technical Recommendations for Grandstands in Modern Stadia*. Berlin Ernst & Sohn, 2008.

Rosenblatt, Arthur. *Building Type Basics for Museums*. Hoboken: Wiley, 2001.

Sawyer, Thomas H. *Facility Planning Design for Health Physical Activity, Recreation, and Sport*, 12th ed. Urbana, IL: Sagamore, 2009.

Chapter 11: Storage Spaces

Heinrich, Martin. *Transport- und Lagerlogistik: Planung, Struktur, Steuerung und Kosten von Systemen der Intralogistik*, 9th ed. Wiesbaden: Springer Vieweg, 2014.

Ten Hompel, Michael, Thorsten Schmidt, and Lars Nagel. *Materialflusssysteme: Förder- und Lagertechnik*, 3rd rev. ed. Berlin: Springer, 2001.

Chapter 12: Technical Equipment Rooms

Grondzik, Walter T., and Alison G. Kwok. *Mechanical and Electrical Equipment for Buildings*, 12th ed. Hoboken: Wiley, 2014.

Pistohl, Wolfram, Christian Rechenauer, and Birgit Scheuerer. *Handbuch der Gebäudetechnik, vol. 2, Heizung, Lüftung, Beleuchtung, Energiesparen*, 8th ed. Cologne: Werner, 2013.

RWE. *Bau-Handbuch*. Frankfurt: EW Medien und Kongresse Buchverlag, 2014.

Trost, Frederick Jerome, and Ifte Choudhury. *Design of Mechanical and Electrical Systems in Buildings*, Upper Saddle River, NJ: Pearson, 2003.

Index

Imprint

Author: Bert Bielefeld, Prof. Dr.-Ing., is an architect, professor of building economics
and construction management at the University of Siegen, and founding partner
of the planning firm bertbielefeld&partner architekten ingenieure, based in Dortmund.

Book concept and editing: Annette Gref

Project management: Annette Gref, Silke Martini

Translation from German into English: David Koralek/ArchiTrans, with assistance from Hartwin Busch

Copy editing: Keonaona Peterson

Drawings: David Hollnack and Viktouria Kezir, with assistance from Katharina Holterhof
and Alexander Pilar
Figure 3.22, page 33 from Zimmermann, Astrid. *Planning Landscape: Dimensions,
Elements, Typologies.* Basel: Birkhäuser, 2015.

Production: Bettina Chang

Layout (basic concept): Hug & Eberlein

Typesetting and cover design: Sven Schrape

Paper: 130 g/m² Amber Graphic

Printing: Kösel GmbH & Co. KG, Altusried-Krugzell

The technical recommendations contained in this book reflect the current state of technology but
expressly require explicit coordination by the responsible specialist planners to ensure compliance
with the applicable and current laws, regulations, and standards of the country concerned. Neither
the author nor the publisher can be held in any way accountable for the design, planning or execution
of faulty work.

Library of Congress Control Number: 2018949845

Bibliographic information published by the German National Library
The German National Library lists this publication in the Deutsche Nationalbibliografie;
detailed bibliographic data are available on the Internet at http://dnb.dnb.de.

ISBN 978-3-0356-1723-8

This publication is also available in a German language edition (ISBN 978-3-0356-1722-1).

© 2018 Birkhäuser Verlag GmbH, Basel
P.O. Box 44, 4009 Basel, Switzerland
Part of Walter de Gruyter GmbH, Berlin/Boston

9 8 7 6 5 4 3 2 1   www.birkhauser.com